Dora Bryan's
Tapestry Tales

Dora Bryan's Tapestry Tales

Dora Bryan

CANTERBURY
PRESS
Norwich

© Dora Bryan and Chris Gidney 2005

First published in 2005 by the Canterbury Press Norwich
(a publishing imprint of Hymns Ancient & Modern Limited,
a registered charity)
St Mary's Works, St Mary's Plain,
Norwich, Norfolk, NR3 3BH

www.scm-canterburypress.co.uk

British Library Cataloguing in Publication data

A catalogue record for this book is available
from the British Library

ISBN 1-85311-621-1

Typeset by Regent Typesetting
Printed and bound by
Biddles Ltd, www.biddles.co.uk

Contents

Acknowledgements

My sincere thanks in helping me write this book must go to: Bill, my wonderful husband; my family for all the love and many experiences they have contributed to my life over the years; Chris for his help in writing, compiling and making sense of all the thoughts and information I threw in his direction. He's a good catcher!; Sally Goring at Christians in Entertainment, who is always ready to listen; my publisher Christine Smith at Canterbury Press for her faith in this book. Christine Odell's Easter prayer, from *Open with God*, published by Inspire, is used with the author's permission. Unless otherwise stated, all Bible quotations are from the Good News Bible and used with permission. I have credited items that were sent to me where possible, but if there are any that should be credited to someone unknown to me, please let me know so that I can correct this in any future edition.

Foreword
by Chris Gidney

Despite the many miles I drive, car accidents have been rare, but the one I encountered that hot summer's day was quite a wallop. It was my first interview day with Dora Bryan for a new and exciting book which we were to share in the creation of. *Tapestry Tales*, Dora's own idea for a title, was something that would encompass her many experiences of life's ups and downs alongside an explanation of how her daily walk with God has enabled her to carry on, even at the worst of times.

As I headed down the A23 near Brighton, a fast blue car overtook me just as the lanes narrowed from two to three at the top of a hill. When it found itself only yards from a line of stationary cars dead ahead, the old Peugeot suddenly swung back in front of mine, narrowly avoiding my front bumper.

I braked quickly and managed to avoid colliding with him by inches, but before I could sit back with any relief I was thrown forwards and then backwards by a massive impact from behind. The driver at my rear had not been so quick to react and I was pushed several yards down the road before we both came to a crumpled stop. I didn't dare look behind me. I had felt and heard the blow that had caused my back wheels to seize up and skid, and I expected there to be no backside of the car left at all.

My first thought was absolute frustration; not only was I going to be late meeting Dora, I may not get there at all. Worst of all, this was the very first day of the book!

Quite shaken, I eventually managed to open my door and climb out. Mercifully, neither I nor the other driver was hurt, but his car was a complete write-off. Then, as I looked back to mine, the immediate thought that ran through my head was that my car was either made of solid steel or had been surrounded by a ring of angels. The back of my Fiat had been pushed forward, up and under the wheels, but with a few strong tugs I managed to pull the crumpled mass of bodywork away. It freed the wheels and almost miraculously, after swapping insurance details with the other driver, I was able, cautiously, to drive away.

Soon I was picking up speed and as all seemed to be well with the car, I decided to carry on and meet Dora. A few hundred yards down the road I reached the tail end of the car jam again. This time I could see the reason for the hold-up. Drivers were slowing down to see the police, fire service and ambulance rescuing the driver of a yellow car that had somehow skidded off the road and turned upside down. It was a sobering sight, because that could have been me. Somehow my accident, although happening at a similar time on the same stretch of road, had been less acute. I felt doubly lucky to be alive and sensed a bigger arm of protection around me.

As I drove on to Brighton, I reflected on how appropriate this experience was to my destination. Dora had been involved in a very serious accident many years before. She also had a very fortunate escape, and her life-and-death experience changed not only her view on life, but her need for God too. Personal crises often have the effect of making us stop and reconsider where we are on the 'Monopoly board' of life.

Dora's life has been one of enormous professional success. However, alongside her great acting achievements Dora has endured a life full of personal hurdles and set-backs. Her logo could easily be the two masks of opposing expressions, one smiling and one frowning, except that I've never seen Dora frown. The interesting thing is that through all the years I have known her, her personal difficulties have never stopped Dora from carrying on in the path that she believes is right. I've never heard her complain about her life, but only feel abundantly grateful for it.

Much of her strength has come from knowing that most exquisite of God's heavenly gifts, laughter. Dora is able to make even the most mundane of subjects completely hilarious. She causes everyone around her to collapse into hysterics with a single word or look, and she is one of the most natural stewards of the gift of laughter that I know.

She also has a strong personal belief in, and experience of, a God who cares about her. She says it is God who has brought her strength, provided inspiration and delivered new hope every step of the way.

My car was eventually repaired, and a few visits to the osteopath soon put my whiplash injury to rights. For Dora too, the sudden events in her life that caused so much pain at the time have been turned here into a living resource of comfort, encouragement, challenge and, of course, laughter.

What has been so exciting about working with Dora on this book is how relevant the Bible is to everyone today, whoever and wherever we are in our lives. The way in which the Bible has jumped out at Dora and me as we have searched the scriptures for connections to daily life today has been truly remarkable, but perhaps not surprising. It's still a living book, and one that God continues to use as he speaks to us on a daily basis.

I know that *Dora Bryan's Tapestry Tales* will be more than a personal insight into one our best-loved actresses; it will be a book that will warm your spirit and ignite your heart too.

Introduction

I've always done needlework of one kind or another, but it was knitting that really got me into trouble. When I was an assistant stage manager, the general dogsbody, training without payment at Oldham Repertory Theatre, one of my jobs was to open and close the curtains, or 'tabs' as we call them in the profession.

As a young girl of 14 it was quite a responsibility. I realized that if I opened them too early the actors wouldn't be ready and it would have been embarrassing to see them taken by surprise. On the other hand, if I closed them too early the audience might not get to see the end of the play. Tricky stuff, and it took me a while to perfect it. However, by the time I had one play sussed, the company were doing another, as the shows changed each week.

Alongside dimming the lights, which was done by putting an iron rod into a bucket of water, I was also in charge of music, playing the records when appropriate music was needed to set the scene. One week they did Ibsen's *Ghosts*, a very gloomy play. It was during World War Two, on a cold and foggy night, that I had watched a few members of the audience through a hole in the side of the curtains. By the time the interval came they all seemed so depressed that I decided they needed cheering up. I'd just bought Joe Loss's 'In the Mood' from a record shop and thought it was the perfect choice to get everyone happy again, so I put it on instead of the usual chamber music. I got a lot of fierce looks from all the actors standing backstage.

I could see that I had cheered everyone up and I was just about to turn the record over and put on 'The Woodchoppers' Ball' when the director came chasing round backstage.

'What have you done, Dora?' Douglas said, fuming.

'I just thought it would lighten the mood a bit,' I said, quivering.

'It's not supposed to be light!' he shouted. 'Whose record is this?'

'Mine,' I admitted.

'Well, you're not playing that again,' he bellowed. Then he snatched it off the turntable and snapped it in half between his hands.

'That was four and sevenpence ha'penny!' was all I could think of to say.

The theatre needed a skeleton for a play once, so they sent me up to Oldham Royal Infirmary to borrow one. When they could see that I was worried how to get it back to the theatre one of the nurses said, 'Why not borrow a wheelchair?'

So I set off down the High Street pushing a wheelchair with a skeleton sitting in it enjoying the ride. Lots of people stared and eventually a policeman came up and asked me where I was going. I said we were going to the theatre. He took one look at the pile of bones and said, 'Well, you're a bit late for that, aren't you, luv?'

Knowing how mischievous I could be, it was a miracle that the acting company ever let me be the prompter, but they did. This was a most important job, for if an actor should 'dry' I was the one who should shout the forgotten line clearly and crisply from the prompt corner of the stage. In those days this happened quite regularly as each actor would be playing a number of roles in different plays each week, while rehearsing completely new ones during the day.

It could be very boring, so while following the script, I took up the habit of knitting. I could knit without my eyes leaving the script and if there was a pause that seemed any longer than necessary I would call out the line, hoping it was loud enough for the actor to hear but soft enough for the audience to miss.

During the play *Pygmalion* one evening, when the character Doolittle was in the middle of delivering his long speech about 'what is morality?', the poor old actor completely dried.

'What?' he shouted towards my direction off-stage.

'What!' I hissed back. I had been told never to give the whole line, just a word to get the actor back on track, to get them going.

'What?' he repeated.

'What!' I hissed back.

'Where's "What"?' he said, having given up and walked briskly over to the prompt corner.

'There's "What",' I said, putting my finger on the right place in the script. The look he gave me as he went back on to continue his speech was one I shall never forget.

It was Douglas Emery, the director, who was keen to get me out of the prompt corner and properly on to the stage, but my young age often restricted this. Maids, old ladies wearing wigs and other such coveted parts were the order of the day. When a production of *St Joan* came along I sighed in despair when yet again I was given the part of a monk. During the long, boring trial scene I would sit alongside the other monks with the cowl over my head for what seemed like hours. One day I discovered I could continue knitting under my monk's habit, and got quite a few inches of a cardigan done that week.

All would have been fine had it not been for the fact that I dropped one of the huge balls of red quick-knit wool as I stood up to leave the stage one night. I think it got tangled around my legs and those of my fellow monks. So from that day on Douglas decided that he really had to give me proper parts.

Throughout my career the knitting continued, despite the fact that at first wool was hard to come by, during the limitations of the war. I got quite adept at undoing something like a sweater and knitting it into something else. Soon I progressed to crochet and from there it was a simple hop to patchwork.

One day I decided to have a go at patchwork quilts. Mother had a dress shop and so she always had bits of spare material I could use. I made a lot of patchwork quilts because they were easy to sew and easy to transport. I've still got one of the first quilts I made, nearly 60 years ago, but it's a bit faded now. By the time I began to make curtains and bed covers my career had taken off and I was starring in a whole range of films as well as shows and reviews around the country.

Even on the opening night of a revue called *Going to Town* in London's West End I was making curtains in my dressing room. Alan Melville, the show's writer, came backstage to see me in the interval and was astonished to see the floor covered in material, with a sewing machine by my side. I was making the pelmets for my new curtains, but this was opening night, remember, the one night I was supposed to be nervous and anxious about the new show and all the critics. Alan just couldn't believe what he saw.

I suppose he had come round to see how I was coping with the first night, as he had written a wonderfully funny script. I played a woman who was visiting a psychiatrist. She was worried because she had a habit of pushing people over and so she had been told to go and see someone in the medical profession. She explains to the psychiatrist how it had all started when she pushed her little brother off the end of the pier in Worthing.

'Well, he was standing on the edge, you see. He was looking down to see if he could see any fish, and I just gave him a push.'

'Didn't your mother or father notice?' asks the bewildered doctor.

'Oh no, because Mum was having her fortune told at Madame Zenobia. I remember because Madame Zenobia had told my mother that there was going to be a family bereavement within a seven. And it was seven weeks later my brother was washed up.'

Then she tells the story of an annual Sunday school outing involving a double-decker bus.

'Where did you go, Miss Manson?' asks the psychiatrist.

'Beachy Head,' she replies. 'I did feel a fool coming home all alone on the top of a double-decker.'

This was because she had pushed everybody over the edge. And so it went on, as this woman regales more and more stories of how and when she pushed people off the edges of things. It amazes me that I can still remember all the lines of this sketch, 40 years or so later.

She even admits that she pushed her father off a precipice on a skiing holiday, and did the same to her mother when invited to afternoon tea on a London department store's roof garden.

'Well, I'm sure it's all your imagination,' the psychiatrist concludes. 'I really don't think you need to worry. Forget the whole thing.'

'You mean to say I'm just imagining the whole thing?'

'Oh yes.'

'Well how much do I owe you?'

'Fifty guineas, please.'

'Oh!' she replies, knowing that 50 guineas is a lot of money.

The woman starts rifling through her handbag, but when she sees the psychiatrist go to stand by the window she runs towards him and pushes him out too.

'Well, I'm so glad it's all in my imagination,' she says, making a speedy exit while the audience are left laughing and clapping. It went a bomb every night.

At the first-night party Alan spent the whole time saying, 'You'll never guess what Dora was doing in the interval – making the curtains for her new house!'

When my mum died in Brighton many years ago she left behind an unfinished tapestry. It was half full of very pretty flowers and it seemed such a shame to just leave it that way. I had never done tapestry before, so I decided that I would just try and copy what she had already started. I managed to pick up the idea pretty quickly and within a few weeks I had it finished and on top of my piano stool. I was very proud of this, and it started me on a journey to make more.

The sad thing about this piano stool was that in 2003 my husband Bill and I decided to get rid of our grand piano because it was taking up too much room in our home, and we never really used it any more. I still needed a rehearsal piano, so we decided to sell the old grand and replace it with a new upright.

I was away from home, up in Yorkshire filming *Last of the Summer Wine*, when the men came to remove the grand piano. When I got back a few days later I went to look for some of my music and discovered that they had taken the piano stool with my tapestry on as well. I immediately telephoned the removal firm, but they said they had no idea where it had gone. I never found it, and the new upright sounded more like a 'hurdy-gurdy'.

I was really downhearted to lose this special piece of work, and I still pray that one day it will turn up somewhere, but it made me determined to keep going with the tapestry. I now enjoy tapestry so much that nearly every chair and cushion cover and each present I give is made in this way. I've just finished a Clarice Cliff design, which involves bold and bright shapes. Another favourite designer is Kaffe Fassett, an expert in needlepoint.

The process is quite simple. I start off with a piece of material with a lot of holes known as a canvas base. I then use a needle and thread to weave a picture. I can have two or three tapestries on the go at once, and depending on my mood I decide each day which one I'm going to work on. I use wool, silks and various threads, and there's a never-ending choice of designs – I've done a lot of cats and gardens and flowers.

But I'm not one just to sit by the fire in the evenings and weave away, I can do it anywhere. On the bus, in a plane, at the cinema, even in the back of a London taxi if I'm in the mood. I can watch a bit of television while pulling the wool through on a tapestry, but it's really become a way of switching off from all the strains and stresses of life, and I have a few of those! I've got a fairly active mind and I always blame this on the early days of my career when perhaps I was over-stimulated by learning all those different roles every week. I've found that tapestry is the solution – it frees up my mind, but gives me a focus too.

It creates good thinking time, when I can reflect on the past or contemplate the future. It's also a fantastic opportunity to talk to God as I pray. Prayer has always been an essential part of my life's journey and my prayers are sometimes so conversational that it seems like I'm not praying at all, but just chatting away to God. Whenever I do this I always come away feeling inspired, with a renewed energy, confidence in myself and trust in God. This is because when life seems like an endless struggle, I have taught myself to sit down alone and try to relax. Then I can be still and let the Lord in to share all my very real problems.

There are as many aspects to tapestry as there are chapters in my own life, and here is a collection of my favourite thoughts, prayers, poems, hymns and stories that often come to mind as I weave away. You can read it from cover to cover, or dip in and out as often as you like. Whatever you decide, I pray that it may be an inspiration to you as it has been for me.

Enjoying the View

In the beginning God created the heavens and the earth.
Genesis 1.1

Tapestry takes me to a different world, away from life's pressures, where I often feel closest to God, but it's his creation which has the biggest impact on me. Living on the seafront at Brighton gives me a special opportunity each day, all day, to appreciate what he has made.

If I get up early enough in the morning I can marvel at the intensity of his sunrise. During the day I can stand open-mouthed at the vastness of his blue ocean and clear sky. In the evening his amazing sunsets over the sea are a sight to behold. And even in the middle of the night, I can sneak out of bed and gaze at his full moon glistening on the water.

He made the most beautiful tapestry of all: the world we live in. Isn't it such a shame when we damage it? I would be heartbroken if someone came into my house and ripped one of my tapestries to shreds.

It's sadder still when its beauty is not properly appreciated. Part of the joy of taking such effort and time over making a tapestry is to watch people's happy reactions when I show them the finished article. I'm delighted when they can take as much joy from it as I did creating it.

I think God must be sad when people don't appreciate what he has made, perhaps even assuming it is all an accident. I would be most upset if someone looked at my handiwork and called it an 'accident'!

In fact, I admire atheists. If they can look at the amazing beauty of the natural world, and then have the confidence to declare that God doesn't exist, then they have more faith than I do!

Of course, God hasn't finished creating. He didn't just stop and take a seat to watch it all happen; he's involved in our lives on a daily basis, and is still in the business of creating.

Perhaps we are all in danger of taking God's creation for granted. Today, I'm going to try and remember to say thank you for every bit of his handiwork I come across. Will you join me?

God's Handiwork

God looked at everything he had made,
and he was very pleased.
Genesis 1.31

This wonderful song was written by Cecil Frances Alexander, and appeared in her book, *Hymns for Little Children*, published in 1848. Alexander is believed to have written the lyrics at Markree Castle, near Sligo, Ireland.

As many hymns, it has certainly stood the test of time, perhaps because it strikes a chord within our own experience and understanding of a God who loves his creation.

For me this hymn conjures up wonderful images of what God has made. It brings back memories of flowers I have seen, mountains I have marvelled at, and rivers I have walked along.

All things bright and beautiful,
All creatures great and small,
All things wise and wonderful,
The Lord God made them all.

Each little flower that opens,
Each little bird that sings,
He made their glowing colours,
He made their tiny wings.

The purple-headed mountain,
The river running by,
The sunset, and the morning
That brightens up the sky.

The cold wind in the winter,
The pleasant summer sun,
The ripe fruits in the garden,
He made them every one.

The tall trees in the greenwood,
The meadows where we play,
The rushes by the water,
To gather every day.

He gave us eyes to see them,
And lips that we might tell
How great is God Almighty,
Who has made all things well.

All things bright and beautiful,
All creatures great and small,
All things wise and wonderful,
The Lord God made them all.

So Far, So Good

No god is like your God,
riding in splendour across the sky,
riding through the clouds
to come to your aid.
Deuteronomy 33.26

At the end of my early morning prayers, before I put the porridge on, I look out of my little kitchen window and say, 'What do you want me to do today, Lord?' Sometimes the least expected instruction comes and I think how clever he is, as it's often something I know I should do.

So far today, God . . .
I've done all right.
I haven't gossiped.
I haven't lost my temper.
Haven't been grumpy, nasty, or selfish.
I'm really glad of that.

But in a few minutes, God,
I'm going to get out of bed; and from then on,
I'm probably going to need a lot of help!
Amen!

Snuggling up to God

❦

As Jesus and his disciples went on their way, he came to a village where a woman named Martha welcomed him in her home. She had a sister named Mary, who sat down at the feet of the Lord and listened to his teaching. Martha was upset over all the work she had to do, so she came and said, 'Lord, don't you care that my sister has left me all the work to do by myself? Tell her to come and help me!'

The Lord answered her, 'Martha, Martha! You are worried and troubled over so many things, but just one thing is needed. Mary has chosen the right thing and it will not be taken away from her.'

Luke 10.38–42

My dogs Lottie and George are well used to the tapestry lifestyle.

'Oh, she's getting out the embroidery now,' I can hear them say when I reach into my drawer or pocket. 'That means we'll be here for a while, then.' Then they snuggle up beside me on the sofa, or at my feet, and wait patiently for me to finish.

I'm sure they would rather go for a walk, chase a cat, or have some more dinner, but for now they are content to settle beside me, their mistress. Their ears prick up as they hear the tugging sounds of the needle and the occasional mumble as I decide which bit to do next. Sometimes they are so happy they drift off to sleep.

I've spent so much of my life trying to please God. 'Don't worry, God,' I'll say. 'I can do that for you!'

Martha was the same. She was so concerned with trying to do what she thought was the right thing that she was missing the opportunity to hear what Jesus had to say. Words that could have a powerful and positive impact on her life.

I must admit that I'm probably more of a 'doer' than a 'listener', so I'm pleased that Jesus didn't actually condemn Martha, he just defended the choice that Mary had made. Nevertheless, I still want to hear what God has to say to me, and my tapestries help me do this. Each day I make sure I spend some time by his side with my ears wide open.

Suffer the Little Children

So Jesus called a child, made him stand in front of them, and said, 'I assure you that unless you change and become like children, you will never enter the Kingdom of heaven. The greatest in the Kingdom of heaven is the one who humbles himself and becomes like this child. And whoever welcomes in my name one such child as this, welcomes me.'

Matthew 18.2–5

When I was small I thought it terribly unfair that God should take obvious delight in making little children suffer. It was only later that I discovered this old English word actually meant 'allow'. It was the opposite of what I thought God was doing. Rather than causing them pain, he wanted his disciples to bring them over to him so that he could bless them.

It always amazes me how children see things so differently. This little set of verses reminds me to take a leaf out of their book from time to time.

When I look at a patch of dandelions, I see a bunch of weeds that are going to take over my yard. My kids see flowers for Mum and blowing white fluff you can wish on.

When I hear music I love, I know I can't carry a tune and don't have much rhythm so I sit self-consciously and listen. My kids feel the beat and move to it. They sing out the words. If they don't know them, they make up their own.

When I feel wind on my face, I brace myself against it. I feel it messing up my hair and pulling me back when I walk. My kids close their eyes, spread their arms and fly with it, until they fall to the ground laughing.

When I pray, I say thee and thou and grant me this, give me that. My kids say, 'Hi, God! Thanks for my toys and my friends. Please keep the bad dreams away tonight. Sorry, I don't want to go to heaven yet. I would miss my Mummy and Daddy.'

When I see a mud puddle I step around it. I see muddy shoes and dirty carpets. My kids sit in it. They see dams to build, rivers to cross, and worms to play with.

I wonder if we are given kids to teach or to learn from? No wonder God loves the little children!

Enjoy the little things in life, for one day you may look back and realize they were the big things.

God's Texts

Oh, how I love your law!
I meditate on it all day long.
Psalm 119.97 (NIV)

Interestingly, I have always been pretty good at learning my lines. This certainly helped in the early days of my acting career, when I was living at home. Often I would arrive home late in the evening after a show and learn a new script through the night. My dad would appear first thing in the morning with a nice strong cup of tea before I went off to rehearsals for the day.

My learning process involves repeating the lines over and over again to myself, parrot fashion, until they're pretty secure in my mind. It's always a bonus if I can arrive at rehearsals with my script memorized. Then I can start concentrating on the movements and characterization straight away, which ultimately gives me more time to work on them.

Living in Brighton means travelling by train to London a lot, which is also useful for learning lines. No reading of newspapers or books for me, just sitting there mumbling behind a script, or looking out of the window going through the lines in my head.

I've often found that memorizing a particular Bible verse has been helpful at times too, just as David is meditating on God's word in Psalm 119. In this one psalm alone, he mentions meditating on God's word more than ten times, so it must have been pretty important to him. He considers that God's word brings healing, comfort and sustenance. 'Your word is a lamp to guide me and a light for my path,' he says in verse 105.

Although I'm hopeless at remembering which book or chapter it comes from, I sometimes hang on to the words of a verse and let them trundle round my mind for days. It can be a sort of therapy, enabling me to remember who is in charge and why I don't need to worry so much.

I also like to copy out verses that mean something to me in the front of my Bible, or every now and then underline them in the text if they pop out at me when I'm reading. I then use these verses to meditate on from time to time. A friend of mine used to drop off to sleep in his armchair. When his grand-children tried to bring him round with, 'Grandpa, you've fallen asleep,' he would jump up, all dozy and with a big smile, and say, 'No, no. Just meditating, my dears!'

Meditating on a Bible verse is a very refreshing experience. Why not choose one today?

Tales of the Unexpected

During the war it was very difficult to find men for the stage as
they were all away fighting. We had to use the ones that were
left, who tended to be too old, or had flat feet or bad eyesight.

We were doing *Jane Eyre* at Oldham Rep and I was playing
Jane. The man who arrived to play Rochester was definitely an
army reject. Harold was very old and had huge pebble glasses
and a wig.

As usual we only had five days to rehearse the new production. Somehow Harold managed to read through his script and
we began to work out the basic movements. For some reason
his trilby always caught my eye – he never took it off. But I had
my own script to learn so I said nothing, and hoped that he
would be all right on the night, as they say.

Unfortunately he wasn't. He hadn't learned his lines very
well and on the first night would pull the script out of his back
pocket from time to time to check where he was.

In the middle of a very dramatic speech, where he was going
on and on at me, the young governess, to marry him, I noticed
that his wig had shifted sideways. During Act Two his false
teeth started moving around, and were never in the place

required for him to talk properly. Added to this, his trousers were becoming wet because of an incontinence problem.

The various movements of his body and trousers continued as he stood opposite me on stage, declaring his undying love and imploring for my hand in marriage.

'Jane, Jane. Will you marry me?'

Perhaps for a moment I looked a little confused, and then I really didn't know whether I was coming or going because all of a sudden a little old lady on the front row stood right up and shouted, 'Don't do it, Dora. He's too old for you!'

I don't remember what happened next, because I was so rigid with nerves, but looking back it was a very funny incident. It reminds me that God wants us to be aware of what is going on around us. After all, we are his witnesses, his hands, his feet and his heart to those he loves.

Staying in Touch

❦

Do all this in prayer, asking for God's help.
Pray on every occasion as the Spirit leads.
For this reason, keep alert and never give up.
Ephesians 6.18

I fell in love when I was just 16. I met Bill outside the gentlemen's toilets on the corner of Star Inn in Oldham. I was waiting for the evening bus home, and Bill asked his friend to ask me whether I was going to the dance at the weekend. During the war we had to clear the theatre before nine o'clock because of air raids, so that meant there was always plenty of time for a dance at the local ballroom, above the Co-op, after I had finished work.

When Bill's friend asked me I looked across at Bill and thought he looked just like the Hollywood star Gregory Peck. As Gregory Peck was someone I was quite keen on, I said 'yes' almost without thinking. The rest is history, because when I met Bill face to face at the dance we both fell instantly in love.

More than 50 years later we are still in love, and our love has grown even more over the years. Sometimes people ask me how I have managed to keep my marriage alive and well in the heady world of showbiz, which is renowned for its infidelity and heartbreak. One of my secrets has been that he has come with me as much as possible on my travels. Always keeping in touch is another. In the days before mobile phones it wasn't as easy as it is today, but calling from a telephone box or hotel room was always important to me.

Friendships, I've discovered, only stay alive if I work on them. If I don't see someone for months at a time, it's all weather talk when we do catch up, but if we've met or kept in touch on a regular basis we can chat away as if we've never been apart.

The same happens when I pray. If I haven't had a chat with God for quite a while I find it's a bit stiff going at first, and I always feel a little guilty. I do try and talk to God most of the time and involve him in my day as much as possible, because I know just how important it is to stay in touch.

The God of History

꩜

Jesus Christ is the same yesterday,
today, and for ever.
Hebrews 13.8

The history of making tapestries stretches right back to ancient Greece, so it's a very old hobby. Tapestries also depict history in the making, such as the earliest stories of Homer's *Odyssey* and *Iliad*, to the famous Bayeux tapestry of the Battle of Hastings, right up to the D-Day tapestry and beyond. Some very old huge, tapestries form wall hangings that are absolutely beautiful. They depict so many happenings throughout humanity's past that they can cover a complete wall. Fortunately for my family I keep to smaller canvases! Even then my husband Bill says, 'No more cushions, please!' – which is why my friends are now getting them.

God is interested in the canvas that depicts our history too. Happily, he remembers all the good bits of my life and, even better, he deletes all the bad bits when I ask him for his forgiveness. The important thing is that history can teach us so much, including how not to make the same mistake twice!

God has been involved with his creation since the beginning. He didn't just start the ball rolling and then sit down on a big throne with his long beard and forget all about us. He's stuck with us from generation to generation.

It's because God was with me in my yesterday, and walks with me in my today, that I can be confident he will guide me in my tomorrow.

If You've Got Something to Say . . .

❦

Kind words are like honey –
sweet to the taste and good for your health.
Proverbs 16.24

I just love some of the humorous notices that people put out-side their churches, don't you? It's good to show those who pass by that Christians have a sense of humour, and perhaps help them understand that church is a joyful place to be. I've seen some funny ones recently, and here's a few of my favourites.

Coincidence is when God does something but chooses to remain anonymous.

Don't put a question mark where God put a full stop.

Don't wait for six strong men to take you to church.

Forbidden fruits create many jams.

God doesn't call the qualified – he qualifies the called.

God loves everyone, but probably prefers 'fruits of the spirit' over 'religious nuts'.

God promises a safe landing, not a calm passage.

If God is your co-pilot – swap seats!

Most people want to serve God, but only in
an advisory capacity.

Prayer: Don't give God instructions – just report for duty!

The task ahead of us is never as great as the power behind us.

The Will of God will never take you where the Grace of God
will not protect you.

A Horrible Accident

❧

I will lie down and sleep in peace,
for you alone, O Lord,
make me dwell in safety.
Psalms 4.8 (NIV)

If I ever want to remind myself of God's work in my family, I only have to remember a serious car accident in Spain when we were all saved. We had just enjoyed a lovely holiday at Jimmy Tarbuck's villa Chez Redez near Marbella, and were on our way to Bilbao to come back on the ferry. Our Mercedes was overloaded with extras from our holiday, including a blow-up dinghy complete with engine. I was sitting in the back with Georgina, nine, and William, who was seven. Daniel was 11 and was sitting in the front seat, and Bill was driving.

I had insisted that we make a slight detour on the way to Granada to see the sights there, although the rest of the family weren't that keen. We had to follow a dangerously winding road with sheer drops to the side, and we were descending at about 20 miles an hour. It was drizzling and I remember looking at a church clock that said ten minutes past four when we went into a skid.

'Look out, Bill,' I shouted as we went right over the edge, down the mountain side. We came to a terrible, crashing halt as we hit a sort of uninhabited croft. The car was upside down and there was silence for some time. The first sound I heard was

Georgina saying, 'I can't get out, Daddy. The door won't open.'

I imagined we were all dead apart from Georgina, but I was eventually pulled out by my feet through a broken window by a passer-by. I had cuts on my face, but the agonizing pain was from my broken ribs and collar bone. I saw William standing at the side of the road wearing a T-shirt that said 'Kiss, Kiss', and passed out.

Daniel and I were put in a little car that pretended to be an ambulance and it rushed us to a clinic at nearby Jaen. Eventually Bill arrived with William and Georgina, and told me that the car was a complete write-off. The police had said we were lucky to be alive.

After some temporary emergency treatment we spent the night in the clinic, though there was no one to look after us. It was usual in those days for friends and family to do the nursing, and the town wasn't equipped for visiting tourists. One piece of comfort came from a local lady who brought me a lettuce and said something to me in Spanish.

I lay on a hard bed praying for help. In the late 1960s we had no travel insurance, and had lost all our papers and money. I asked God if he could send a helicopter over and take us home from this mess. Our agent back in the UK sent over some air tickets, so we could fly from Madrid back to London.

We were put in a taxi to take us to the railway station at Jaen, with handkerchiefs and bandages everywhere, but when on the way two cars collided and exploded in front of us I didn't feel I could take any more. We stopped at a nearby hotel and called a doctor. He gave me a shot of morphine to kill the pain.

We eventually got to Madrid and flew home. To say that we were mightily grateful is quite an understatement. I definitely believe God had his hands on us, even though I didn't realize it at the time.

Finders Keepers

Sometimes I lose things. And I don't mean my head! I've
recently lost a very precious tapestry, which took me the whole
of one year's *Last of the Summer Wine* filming to complete. I'm
hoping it will turn up somewhere but the fact that it remains
lost reminds me about the stories in the Bible of the lost coin
and the lost sheep.

I must admit I was pretty lost until I found God. This happened through working on a film with Cliff Richard. I was
appearing in *Hello, Dolly!* at the Theatre Royal, Drury Lane in
London and was asked out to lunch by Cliff and a film director
called James Collier. They took me to a very posh restaurant in
Covent Garden called The Garden Restaurant, so I knew they
had something important to talk to me about!

'I'd love you to be in a new film I'm making called *Two
A Penny*,' explained Cliff. 'It's being produced by the Billy
Graham Organization.'

'Oh,' I said. 'What part do you want me to play?'

'My mum!' smiled Cliff.

'Ooo, that's nice,' I replied, wondering if it really was. 'And what sort of fees are we talking about?'

'I'm afraid there are no fees,' piped up James. 'Only expenses.'

'But it's a good storyline,' added Cliff quickly. 'I'm a drug dealer.'

I looked at him with wide eyes and carried on sipping my soup in wonderment. 'I do get rescued, though,' he added speedily.

Well, it was such a lovely lunch, and they were such good company, how could I refuse? Little did I know that God had a plan lurking beneath all of this!

I gradually met everyone involved in the production and they all seemed such nice people, it almost felt unreal. I knew they were mostly Christians, but at that time I thought that was just a title anyone in England was born with. It didn't really mean anything.

Billy Graham's wife, Ruth, and one of her children came to see me in *Hello, Dolly!* and Ruth came backstage afterwards. She gave me a present – a little notebook in which to write down all the funny things that my children were saying as they grew up. I've still got it somewhere.

When we started filming it was just lovely working with such nice people. After a few days one of the crew sidled up to me and said, 'What d'ya think of it all, Dora? There always seems to be prayer going on in one corner of the set or other.'

I didn't mind at all. In fact, I started to pop in to my local Christian bookshop in Brighton and buy little booklets and tracts about Christianity. I suppose I was quite intrigued by the whole thing. Somehow the religion that the cast were display-ing wasn't just confined to church on a Sunday morning. I could see it was a sort of living faith that made a difference to them each day, and I wanted to know more.

The filming ended and everyone seemed pleased with the result. *Two A Penny* became a sort of Christian cult classic. Next I was whisked up to Liverpool with *Hello, Dolly!*, but in the first week there I went down with the most awful flu, and I had to take the Saturday matinee off. The stage manager, Tony Hardman, who has since become a good friend of ours, helped Bill take the children out ice skating for the afternoon, to give me some extra rest. It was so cold they could even have skated on the sea, and snow laid thick everywhere.

After a bit of a doze, there was a knock on my door. I opened it to see a tall dark figure standing there.

'Cliff gave me your address,' the man explained, 'and asked me to pop in to see you.'

I remember Cliff calling me to ask if it was all right if a friend of his came to see me, but I'd forgotten about it since. Although I felt pretty unwell, something inside me said that this was a special visit, almost an angelic one. I soon learned that this was Max Wigley, a retired canon who was also the theatre chaplain.

There was something about Max I was drawn to. He didn't push religion down my throat, as perhaps I had expected, so it was easy for me to be the one asking all the questions. He was very good at answering all my odd queries. Soon we were spending several mornings a week reading the Bible and praying together. All this Christianity lark finally started to make sense, and it wasn't long before I was down on my knees asking God into my life.

In the Bible story of the lost coin, it probably seems silly that the woman who still had nine other coins bothered to search for the one that was lost, but she did. We are all individually precious to God, and he makes special efforts to seek us out. He sent Cliff and Max, and many others too, to make sure I wasn't lost for long, and help me on my way. So I'm glad I've found God. Or did he find me? Well, whatever. I'm just going to make sure I don't lose him!

Do Seagulls Worry?

ॐ

This is why I tell you not to be worried about the food and drink you need in order to stay alive, or about clothes for your body. After all, isn't life worth more than food? And isn't the body worth more than clothes? Look at the birds: they do not sow seeds, gather a harvest and put it in barns; yet your Father in heaven takes care of them! Aren't you worth more than birds? Can any of you live a bit longer by worrying about it?

Matthew 6.25–27

There are two cheeky seagulls that often sit on my roof and peer over the edge into the window of my sun balcony below. If I'm sitting there doing my tapestry, I always notice when they pop their heads over to look at me with a glint in their eye. I have been known to put bread out for them and they may have spread the word to their mates, because it's starting to be a regular occurrence. I wonder if seagulls worry. Probably not.

I worry, but then sometimes I see people who are professional worriers. Even if they won the Lottery or had all their problems solved, they would still find something to worry about.

The Bible seems to be clear about God not wanting us to worry, because he knows just how harmful it can be. In fact, God is so adamant that we should be at peace that the Bible says 'Do not fear' in one form or another 366 times. That's one for every day of the year, and one left over for leap year! So every time a worry pops up into my mind now, I try and hear his voice saying, 'Don't worry, Dora!'

Here's a prayer by Alec J. Langford:

Dear God,

From our world of worry and strife we call on thee. From the ills of mind and body we pray for relief. From the gnawing of uncertainty of the future, deliver us to thoughts of hope.

We rejoice in, celebrate, and experience with gratitude painless and happy days, encouragement received and tasks achieved, work to do, friends to love, loads to lift, hope to share.

Amen.

It's Behind You!

❦

Surely goodness and love will follow me
all the days of my life,
and I will dwell in the house of the Lord
for ever.
Psalm 23.6 (NIV)

I love pantomime. It's special for me in three ways. First, because it's performed at the time when we celebrate the birth of Christ. Then because it's an opportunity to bring families together. Finally because it's just such fun!

My son Daniel used to be a stage manager, and I always enjoyed the opportunity to work with him. When we were doing *Cinderella* together it was Daniel's job to look after the ponies for the transformation scene. I would stand in one corner of the stage waving my wand, while flashes went off left, right and centre, and Daniel would lead the ponies on. There was always a brush and a pan handy, as the ponies were never able to time their toilet arrangements conveniently. One night, one of them decided to do a huge plop on stage. Florrette, I think her name was.

As the Fairy, I had to ignore all this, but I couldn't help noticing that the plop was glistening. Florrette was a very greedy pony and she used to eat the silver tinsel from Cinderella's coach while waiting in the wings for her entrance. I realized that what she had nibbled during the matinee was now making its appearance in the evening and sparkling under the lights.

When the children in the audience shout out 'It's behind you!' I just love it. It reminds me of the verse from Psalm 23 says that 'goodness and love will follow me', and that from time to time I should look over my shoulder and remember what God has done in my life. It's too easy to forget the times when God has done this thing or that. When I think back I see how God has worked in my life in the past, and this gives me something to hang on to when I'm going through a rough patch.

So stop for a moment and look behind you. You'll be amazed, encouraged and inspired.

Patience Required Please

❦

They refused to obey; they forgot all you did; they forgot the miracles you had performed. In their pride they chose a leader to take them back to slavery in Egypt. But you are a God who forgives; you are gracious and loving, slow to be angry. Your mercy is great; you did not forsake them.

Nehemiah 9.17

Creating a tapestry is quite a long process and can take many weeks or even months to complete. It requires a lot of patience. Oddly, although God seems to have a lot of patience with us, why is it we don't seem able to do the same for him?

I have a friend who gets very low and lonely. There is so little I can do to help, but I *can* pray for her. I did ask her once whether she could talk to God about it. She said she had done so, but then nothing had happened.

'Well, it doesn't happen all at once,' I said. 'He's not a magician.'

We're so impatient sometimes, aren't we? We live in such an instant world that we expect everything on the table in front of us immediately. Not only do we want immediate answers for ourselves, we also want them for friends and family. I know wives who have prayed for a very long time that their husbands will find God. I've been praying for my friend for 17 years now and I expect I shall continue to do so. I know that God will give me the patience I need. Indeed, he promised that the fruit of his Spirit within me would produce love, joy, peace, patience and a lot more besides.

A Theology of Failure

The Lord turned round and looked straight at Peter, and Peter remembered that the Lord had said to him, 'Before the cock crows tonight, you will say three times that you do not know me.' Peter went out and wept bitterly.

Luke 22.61–62

Although I live with my family and two Tibetan terriers on the seafront in Brighton I am Lancashire born and bred, as is my husband Bill. My distinctive voice and accent often attracts attention, so occasionally I have to keep my mouth shut if I want to be anonymous. Even after ten years in London and 45 years in Brighton my accent hasn't changed and is unusual, to say the least, for the south coast, though I can put on a posh voice if I have to.

At one point in my life I started drinking, in an effort to cope with the pressure of being in the entertainment business and running a home and family at the same time. It was the worst thing I could have done, because rather than create a way of escape, it just tied me to an addiction that made me a prisoner.

It was a terrible dependence and one which crept up on me, particularly as the showbiz world is a very social profession to be in. I was away from home quite a lot and often sat alone in my hotel room after the show. For a while I stopped, though, and became completely teetotal for three years, but then I went on tour with an actress who loved drinking champagne. I tried to kid myself that I could stick to non-alcoholic champagne, which was possible to buy in certain places, but before long I was back on the real thing again. It took several months back home to sort myself out again.

I've appreciated and valued the support that Alcoholics Anonymous have given me – after all, I've been a member of AA for 24 years. But at the end of the day, I know that it's really up to me. I know that God gives strength, and help too, but sometimes I think he is also keen to see me make the effort to help myself.

One thing I've noticed is that the Bible is full of people who have struggled and failed with issues. Noah was a drunk. Jacob was a liar. Moses couldn't talk. Gideon was afraid. Rahab was a prostitute. David had an affair and was a murderer. Elijah was suicidal, and Peter denied Christ. If God could use all these failures, then there's hope for me!

Lightening the Load

❧

Elijah was afraid, and fled for his life; he took his servant and went to Beersheba in Judah. Leaving his servant there, Elijah walked a whole day into the wilderness. He stopped and sat down in the shade of a tree and wished he would die. 'It's too much, Lord,' he prayed. 'Take away my life; I might as well be dead!'

1 Kings 19.3–4

Depression is a most awful thing to suffer from. I am very sympathetic to those who struggle with it on a daily basis because I have had experience of it myself at times. Today, depression is recognized as an illness, but this doesn't really make you feel any better when you are in the middle of 'the black storm'.

Depression has taken over my whole life from time to time. It has this terrible habit of creeping up on me, so I'm never prepared for it when it strikes. The first time I experienced this black, black hole was three months after I lost my first baby, after two miscarriages. I'm told that both exhaustion and success can also be triggers, two things that are often closely associated with show business.

There are several types of depression, but mine necessitates an escape from the world, and so hospital seems the best place to be. It creates a space of my own where I can allow my mind to unwind. It's interesting that most of the time I'm not recognized by any of the other residents, often because they are so locked up in themselves. So it's quite a relief that I'm free to be myself, and I don't have to perform in any way.

It's a sort of oasis particularly because the one I've been to is a Christian nursing home, which specializes in depression and associated problems. I'm glad to say they don't throw religion at the residents, but simply provide a spiritually relaxing atmosphere that feels safe and comfortable. My family can visit whenever they want.

I can put my trust in the doctors there and I've even had electric shock therapy there. I found the ECT experience actually less frightening than going to the dentist. I travelled in a minibus to another hospital with five other patients. When we arrived at the clinic, I even offered to go first, perhaps to get it over with, or perhaps to try and show the others that it wasn't anything to worry about. The charity Mind estimates about 20,000 people a year receive ECT in England and Wales.

After a shot of Valium in my arm I was asleep and then it felt I was only out for a few minutes before the nurse was asking me if I wanted a cup of tea. I woke up with a headache and went back to the nursing home and straight to bed, but I felt quite a lot better the next day.

The doctors sometimes put me on a course of drugs which help to balance out the chemical reactions occurring in my body. I read in a medical book about lithium, a salt-based drug sometimes used to level out the mood of the patient. When I asked my doctor about it he said he wouldn't use it in my case because it would level me out so much that I could lose all my creativity. As a performer it's this creativity that I rely on to work. I still have to take a very small dose of antidepressant from time to time, but I have found that the best way to deal with depression is to hand myself over to God each time. It's at my most vulnerable moments that I know without a doubt that I can completely rely on him.

I can usually see a 'light at the end of the tunnel', but as a Christian I still sometimes feel ashamed to admit to depression. I have to remind myself that it is an illness, and one even mentioned in the Bible, so God must understand.

Although rare these days, a bout of depression can last for several months, but I really am always ready to 'let go and let God'. It's the only way.

Giving It to God

As I was with Moses, so I will be with you;
I will never leave you nor forsake you.
Be strong and courageous . . .
Joshua 1.5–6 (NIV)

It's fascinating to read that some medical experts now admit that prayer seems to have the power to heal. When depression strikes, prayer can be the last thing on your mind. But prayer goes straight to your unconscious, where it will not be stopped by the negative thinking so commonly found in a state of despair. Here is a prayer from *Everyday Prayers* to use when you are facing depression:

Lord, there are shadows at the edge of my heart,
the darkness creeps nearer, enemies lurk there, too vague
to be resisted.
I can't think straight, logic has deserted me,
I fear my dreams, and dread waking early:
Help me, Lord.
May I feel your strength beneath me when I fear that I am
sinking.
May your light scatter the darkness where fear hides.
Bring me out to daylight and resurrection.

Taking a Risk

❦

Once there was a man who was about to go on a journey; he called his servants and put them in charge of his property. He gave to each one according to his ability: to one he gave five thousand gold coins, to another two thousand, and to another he gave one thousand. Then he left on his journey. The servant who had received five thousand coins went at once and invested his money and earned another five thousand. In the same way the servant who had received two thousand coins earned another two thousand. But the servant who had received one thousand coins went off, dug a hole in the ground, and hid his master's money.

Matthew 25.14–18

It's all very well having a nice new tapestry to make, but if I leave the wool in the drawer, the needle in my workbox and the picture in its packet it will never get done.

One of the most exciting parts of doing a tapestry is choosing the next project. Will it be a landscape or a picture of a sweet little dog? A bird in the sky, or a beautiful building?

There's always a risk involved, though. Will I have time to do it? Can I battle and win over my guilt because there may be other seemingly more important things I should be doing? Will I actually be able to complete it? Will I make mistakes and have to start all over again? There's only one way to find out. Just get on and do it.

So, with the canvas on my lap, I start to weave away. Slowly but surely it begins to take shape and my picture eventually comes to life. I've discovered it's the same with God. He's not interested in us staying in our 'packets'. He wants to see us get out and enjoy the life he has given. I've seen some Christians be so scared of 'getting it wrong' that it almost stops them from doing anything more risky than going to church on a Sunday morning. God wants us to take risks.

It takes a risk just to be a Christian. I'm sometimes thought of as a bit 'dotty' because I believe in Christ. Though I have to say I think it's harder and more peculiar *not* to believe in him after all the evidence he's given us.

It often takes a risk to achieve success in a career and I've taken plenty of those in my time. That song I recorded about The Beatles, 'All I want for Christmas is a Beatle', could have been the biggest embarrassment of my career. Today it's still hailed as a classic piece of pop history.

God can use us more if we are already walking in some direction than if we are sitting down in an armchair waiting for him to carry us. So don't bury your talents today; risk taking them out, using them, and see where God will take you.

The Odd Job Man

Happy are those who know they are spiritually poor;
The Kingdom of heaven belongs to them!
Happy are those who mourn;
God will comfort them!
Happy are those who are humble;
they will receive what God has promised!
Happy are those whose greatest desire is to do what God requires;
God will satisfy them fully!
Happy are those who are merciful to others;
God will be merciful to them!
Happy are the pure in heart;
they will see God!

Matthew 5.3–8

Mr Sackett was a sweet little man who smoked roll-ups and wore a flat cap just like Andy Capp. Bill and I loved him because he was so simple and straightforward and able to turn his hand to anything that needed doing. I don't know where we found him, but he was a very useful little man.

'How much do we owe you, Mr Sackett?' said Bill after a job he had completed one day.

'Oooo well, whatever you think,' came his reply.

'Well, we normally pay people by the hour,' said Bill.

'Oooo, you can't do that with me,' said the honest little man. 'I'm a slow worker!'

One week I made a huge pair of curtains for our home in Barnes. I bought the heavy, red material from a display of fabrics at Barkers of Kensington, one of the big department stores in town. I gradually sewed them together, with pleats, swirls and a grand pelmet. I was most proud with the finished product, but not as pleased as Mr Sackett. Once he had fixed the curtains up to the runner complete with pulleys to open and close them he stood back with his mouth open and watched as the red material swished back and forwards. 'Ooooo, Dora!' he declared. 'It's just like the Odeon!'

Eventually he became my driver, and would wait for me at the stage door after every show in order to take me to Victoria Station. The only problem was that although he was very friendly he was a bit rough and ready for all the stage-door fans who assembled after the show to ask for an autograph.

'Make way! Make way for Miss Dora,' he would say with a fag hanging out of the corner of his mouth and a shabby raincoat covering an ill-fitting suit.

My agent, 'Binky' Beaumont, saw all this one night and decided it wasn't an acceptable image for a leading actress in the West End. He insisted Mr Sackett be replaced with someone more appropriate and I ended up with two very prim and proper female chauffeurs complete with immaculate grey uniforms.

They seemed to be quite proud of themselves and their job and herded me around from place to place with so much false dignity that I felt distinctly uncomfortable. They hated me popping into the pub across the road from the theatre to have a quick shandy with the rest of the cast after the show and would stand at the door, looking at their watches and announcing, 'Time's getting on, Miss Bryan!'

It was heartbreaking to let Mr Sackett go, because for all the professionalism and polish of the lady chauffeurs, I preferred our pal Mr Sackett any day.

The Bayeux Tapestry

❦

Gideon built an altar to the Lord there
and named it 'The Lord is Peace'
(It is still standing . . .)
Judges 6.24

I love looking at other tapestries. Of course the most famous one is the Bayeux, which was first recorded in 1476 when it was mentioned in the cathedral treasury at Bayeux as 'a very long and narrow hanging on which are embroidered figures and inscriptions comprising a representation of the conquest of England'.

The Bayeux Tapestry was probably commissioned in the 1070s by Bishop Odo of Bayeux, half-brother of William the Conqueror. It's over 70 metres long and some historians argue that it was actually embroidered in Kent. The original tapestry is on display at Bayeux in Normandy, France.

In the nineteenth century a woman named Elizabeth Wardle had the idea to make the replica Bayeux Tapestry. She was a skilled embroiderer and her husband, Thomas Wardle, was a leading silk industrialist. Elizabeth Wardle researched the Bayeux Tapestry by visiting Bayeux in 1885. The aim was to make a full-sized and accurate replica of the Bayeux Tapestry 'so that England should have a copy of its own'.

Thirty-five women members of the Leek Embroidery Society worked under Elizabeth Wardle's direction. This ambitious project was completed in just over a year. As well as members from Leek in Staffordshire, women from Derbyshire, Birmingham, Macclesfield and London took part. Each embroiderer stitched her name beneath her completed panel.

Over the next ten years the tapestry was put on display in towns and cities across Britain and it even travelled to Germany and America. It was finally purchased by a former Mayor of Reading, where it is now displayed.

The tapestry depicts the famous battle of 1066, which even I can remember from my school days was about William the Conqueror leading the Normans across the English Channel and defeating the English King, Harold, at the Battle of Hastings. William then became King of England. The Bayeux Tapestry was created soon afterwards to record the events of William's victory.

It is thought that the original Bayeux Tapestry was crafted by a group of nuns. Perhaps they were concerned to mark this great point in history and ensure that it wasn't forgotten. We all have significant moments in our personal histories too. Some people like to keep a diary, some like to paint pictures, or sculpt, while others use photographs as a way of recording their past. I like the idea of a prayer diary where requests and answers are recorded, enabling the owner to look back and recall how God was in each step in their lives.

In the Bible people built altars in the open when they wanted to remember and worship a particular act of God. I suppose the greatest form of remembrance today is Holy Communion, which is a very practical reminder of what God did to rescue us from ourselves.

It's so important to have some way of marking those important moments in our lives. What's yours?

Abide with Me

Abide in me, and I in you.
As the branch cannot bear fruit of itself,
except it abide in the vine;
no more can ye, except ye abide in me.
John 15.4 (KJV)

'Abide with me' is one of my all-time favourite hymns, because my lovely mum used to play it to me on the piano. I really like the tune as it's so easy to remember and hum as I go about my day. The words were written by Henry Francis Lyte in 1847 – at a time of great sorrow as he was dying of tuberculosis. He used to love to sit and watch the setting sun, just as I do now. This was his inspiration, and as the last golden ray faded, he took some paper and began to pen the verses which have since gone all over the earth.

Lyte finished the hymn on the Sunday he gave his farewell sermon in the parish he served for many years. The next day he left for Italy, to try to regain his health. He never got to Italy, though; he died in Nice in the south of France three weeks after writing these words.

Over 150 years later the bells of his church, All Saints in Lower Brixham, Devon, ring out 'Abide with me' daily. The hymn was sung at the wedding of King George VI, and at the wedding of his daughter, the future Queen Elizabeth II.

'Abide' is a funny old English word, one that we don't use

much these days. Perhaps it has lost its real meaning a little. In the dictionary abide means 'remain, stay, continue, stop, linger, rest'. All the things that I like to do when life gets too much and all I can manage to do is just sit and relax with God at my side.

Abide with me; fast falls the eventide;
The darkness deepens; Lord, with me abide.
When other helpers fail, and comforts flee,
Help of the helpless, O abide with me!

Swift to its close ebbs out life's little day;
Earth's joys grow dim; its glories pass away;
Change and decay in all around I see;
O Thou who changest not, abide with me!

Not a brief glance I beg, a passing word;
But as Thou dwell'st with Thy disciples, Lord,
Familiar, condescending, patient, free.
Come not to sojourn, but abide with me.

Come not in terrors, as the King of kings,
But kind and good, with healing in Thy wings,
Tears for all woes, a heart for every plea –
Come, Friend of sinners, and thus bide with me.

Thou on my head in early youth didst smile;
And, though rebellious and perverse meanwhile,
Thou hast not left me, oft as I left Thee,
On to the close, O Lord, abide with me.

I need Thy presence every passing hour.
What but Thy grace can foil the tempter's power?
Who, like Thyself, my guide and stay can be?
Through cloud and sunshine, Lord, abide with me.

Operation Overlord

❧

*The greatest love a person can have for his friends
is to give his life for them.*
John 15.13

Another famous tapestry that records a major event in human history is the Overlord Embroidery. It's the centrepiece of the D-Day Museum in Portsmouth and shows in stunning detail the progress of Operation Overlord, otherwise known as D-Day. It was commissioned by Lord Dulverton of Batsford as a tribute to the sacrifice and heroism of those who took part, and its inspiration came from the Bayeux Tapestry.

The designer, Sandra Lawrence, first prepared thumbnail sketches using wartime photographs for reference. The advisory board included a retired senior officer from each of the services, dubbed the 'three wise men'! Once the sketches were approved, Sandra painted 34 full-sized watercolours, one for each of the panels. These original watercolours now hang in the Pentagon in Washington.

Pieces of material matching the colours and shades in the paintings were sewn onto linen to create appliqué panels. More than 50 different materials were used, including fabrics taken from uniforms and headgear of those involved in the three services. It took four years to complete and is the largest work of its kind in the world, 272 feet in length.

Lord Dulverton, in his speech at the unveiling, explained

that he had commissioned the Overlord Tapestry to be a tribute not to war itself, but to those who sacrificed their lives to win us our freedom. 'If, in the years ahead, I can bring home to succeeding generations the message of sacrifice and selflessness displayed by those who took part in Overlord, it will have achieved more than I could ever have dared for. We, with all our troubles that beset our world, lead our lives for good or ill with freedom still to make some degree of choice. We tend to forget that this freedom would not be with us still, had evil triumphed in those days.'

I like to reflect on those who gave their lives for peace, but also to remember the ultimate sacrifice; the one that Jesus made in order to overcome evil once and for all. To me he is the greatest 'Over-Lord'.

Reach for the Top

❦

A gentle answer quietens anger, but a harsh one stirs it up.
When wise people speak, they make knowledge attractive, but
stupid people spout nonsense.
Proverbs 15.1–2

There are so many voices clamouring for our attention these days. One thing I've learned over the years is to try and close my ears to other people's tendencies to be overnegative or pessimistic. This little story that was sent me explains why:

There once was a bunch of tiny frogs who arranged a climbing competition. The goal was to reach the top of a very high tower. A big crowd had gathered around the tower to see the race and cheer on the contestants.

The race began, but none in the crowd really believed that the tiny frogs would reach the top of the tower.

'Way too difficult!' said one.

'Not a chance they will succeed,' said another.

The tiny frogs began collapsing with exhaustion, one by one. Except for some, that is, who in a fresh spurt of energy seemed to be climbing higher and higher.

The crowd continued to yell: 'It is too difficult! No one will make it!'

More tiny frogs got tired and gave up.

But one continued, higher and higher and higher. This one wouldn't give up! Soon all the other frogs had given up, except for this one, who after a strong final effort eventually reached the top of the tower.

All the other frogs wanted to know how their friend had managed to reach the top when they couldn't. They wondered how the tiny frog had found the strength to reach the unreachable goal.

'Because I'm deaf,' he said.

He hadn't heard the negative shouts and cries from the crowd. He had simply listened to his own heart.

Corpsing

❧

Despite its name, corpsing has nothing to do with death, unless it's a reference to the fact that if you start laughing uncontrollably on stage you could 'die' in the theatrical sense!

Described as 'a form of hysteria in which an actor breaks into uncontrollable fits of inappropriate laughter at serious moments', corpsing has plagued many careers including mine. Two colleagues of mine, Kenneth Branagh and Dame Judi Dench, are known as two of the worst in the business and were even once kicked off the set of Ibsen's *Ghosts* because of their helpless giggles. Amanda Barrie, Richard Wattis and I were in the comedy *Six of One* and we were corpsing so often that the stage manager had threatened to bring the curtain down. On one occasion we were in a fit of giggles and I saw him in the wings shaking his fist at us. It only made things worse. When the hooks on my dress got caught on Dickie's uniform he had to follow me everywhere around the stage and eventually we all collapsed in a heap of laughter.

Sometimes actors find that corpsing is a natural way of relieving tension, especially if it's been a long day of rehearsal or recording, or if the piece has been a very dramatic and emotionally draining one to perform.

I'm quite a bad corpser, and once I get the giggles it's very hard to stop, even if I'm on live television or on stage during a play. Blowing my front teeth out during Noel Coward's play *Peace in Our Time* with Bernard Lee was one of those memorable occasions!

Two of my teeth had just been crowned by the dentist and I was proudly showing them off to everyone backstage. They were a twenty-first birthday present from my father. Later, I was on stage facing Bernard and starting to deliver my lines, when disaster struck. First one tooth blew out, then as I was looking around wondering where my £50 tooth had flown to, another one went. Fifty years ago £50 was a huge amount of money!

And now the stakes had doubled to £100. Bernard's eyes started to scour the stage. He was hoping to see where the teeth had landed so that they could be rescued in the interval. However, it was his eyes that made me laugh, because they were darting everywhere, all over the place. It took me some while to regain control of myself. We found the missing teeth, but every night after that it took all the energy and discipline I could muster not to break into laughter again when we reached that same scene. I think I managed to get through by avoiding Bernard's eyes at that particular point.

I remember another play when I had to be padded up to the nines to make me look fat. It was rep, so there was no money for real padding made with proper straps. I just had to stuff some cushions into a very large pair of knickers. Unfortunately in the middle of my scene the knicker elastic suddenly broke and cushions fell to the ground one by one as I walked around. It must have looked as if I was laying eggs!

The rest of the cast couldn't believe their eyes and did everything they could to try and smother their laughter. By the end of the scene I was desperately clutching the last two remaining cushions before making a quick exit and bursting into hysterical laughter in the wings. Whatever the audience thought of it all I hate to think, but it cheered us all up no end. Cheerfulness, joy, happiness, fun, laughter. All words that I believe God created just for us.

Jesus the Actor

❧

As they came near the village to which they were going, Jesus acted as if he were going farther; but they held him back saying, 'Stay with us; the day is almost over and it is getting dark.' So he went in to stay with them.

He sat down to eat with them, took the bread, and said the blessing; then he broke the bread and gave it to them. Then their eyes were opened and they recognized him, but he disappeared from their sight.

Luke 24.28–31

I've often been told that God understands each and every one of us, but surely he couldn't really know what it was like to be an actor? That's how doubtful I was until I stumbled across the amazing verse above.

In this version it says that Jesus 'acted'. He must have been pretty good at it, too, because the others he was walking with were so convinced he was going to leave them that they had to use all their persuasive powers to get him to stay!

The more I think about it the more I realize just how much Jesus used his communication skills to draw people to God. For example, he kept 4,000 men plus their wives and families spellbound all day long. He didn't use a microphone but must have been easy to listen to, and who knows, he may have used his disciples in comical sketches to illustrate some of his humorous stories. He kept his audience enthralled for so long

[55]

that he had to provide an impromptu, miraculous feast, out of a few loaves and fish.

Jesus also knew what it was like to be a celebrity. Everywhere he went, people followed him and asked him for things. I know what that's like too. It can be wonderfully reassuring at times, and horribly inconvenient at others.

Jesus may not have appeared on stage. He may not have known what it was like to speak someone else's lines or wear funny costumes, but he understands enough to know what life is like for me.

He understands you, too. If you were to spend some time thinking through what you know of Jesus, and flicking through the New Testament reading about his life, I'm certain you would find similarities between him and your own experiences. It's because he cares, because he wants you to know that he really understands you, and because he loves you so much.

God's Timing

> *There is a time for everything . . .*
> *a time to be born and a time to die,*
> *a time to plant and a time to uproot . . .*
> *a time to weep and a time to laugh,*
> *a time to mourn and a time to dance . . .*
> *a time to be silent and a time to speak . . .*
> Ecclesiastes 3.1–7 (NIV)

If there is one skill every performer needs, be it actor, comedian, singer or musician, it is timing. Without timing the line doesn't make sense, the gag won't work, and the music sounds terrible.

In rep there was very little time to learn our lines, let alone read and understand the whole play, so we would underline what we had to learn and forget about the rest. This meant that if it was a small part I sometimes wouldn't know the context or direction of the play. This is probably why on more than one occasion I have gone on at the wrong time. I would listen for my cue, hear something that sounded about right, and go on, only to find that I was too early.

I would know instantly that I was in the wrong place because of the strange looks I got from the other actors.

'I . . . er . . . I . . . um,' I would splutter with my mind working overtime to find a way to cover my mistake, 'I've got something to tell you, but it'll wait. I'll come back later,' and off I'd go.

When I was in Zimbabwe once and my son Daniel was my stage manager I was doing a very quick change in my dressing room when my zip stuck. It wouldn't go up or down.

'Miss Bryan, your call please,' came Daniel's voice over the backstage tannoy.

'Miss Bryan, your call *please*,' he repeated, a little more urgently.

'Miss Bryan, your call please!' By now the voice was getting hysterical.

Then came, 'FORGET IT, MUM. YOU'RE OFF!'

On the other hand, I've found God's timing to be perfect, even on those occasions when it didn't really seem like it at the time.

God's Gobbledegook

✥

For the eyes of the Lord are on the righteous
and his ears are attentive to their prayer.
1 Peter 3.12 (NIV)

I do have the strangest, silliest conversations in the street sometimes, particularly with people who get me mixed up with other
actresses like Beryl Reid, Joan Sims and Thora Hird.

One day I was in an art gallery in London filling in some
spare time before seeing my agent. I was looking around at the
lovely paintings when a man in a smart morning suit saw me
staring at a very small Lowry.

'It's lovely, isn't it?' he said to me.

'Oh yes,' I agreed. 'How much do you think that would be to
buy?' I said trying to make polite conversation.

'Oh, about seventy-five,' he said.

'Well, seventy-five pounds isn't bad, I suppose,' said I.

'Thousands!' he corrected.

'Oh dear. Yes, of course. Too much for me, though.'

'Oh, come on, Dame Thora, you can afford it!'

Another time I was struggling with my luggage at King's
Cross on my way to film *Last of the Summer Wine*, and a porter
kindly loaded my cases on to the train for me. When I pulled
out a £5 note to tip him he said, 'Oh no, no, no. I couldn't pos-
sibly take that, Dame Thora. I know what it's like. I've had two
hip replacements myself!'

Sometimes I think my prayers are a bit like those people; a tad muddled, jumbled and mixed-up. I'm not always sure what I'm asking or saying, and worried that God might consider my requests silly. I'm just so grateful that God fluently knows, speaks and understands every language he has created, even my chaotic, funny prayers.

Drying

The Lord said to him,
'Who gives man his mouth? . . .
It is I, the Lord.
Now, go!
I will help you to speak and I will tell you what to say.'

Exodus 4.11–12

If there is one nightmare all performers have, it's forgetting one's lines – or drying, as we call it in the business.

Even worse is having to keep talking when someone is 'off'. This happened to me during a recent tour of *The Importance of Being Earnest*. I was on stage, in the middle of the tea scene, waiting for the entrance of the Canon, when he just didn't arrive. At first I didn't know what to talk about but then I ad-libbed quite a long time about lemon drizzle cake. I even gave the audience the recipe for lemon drizzle cake. Why this cake came to mind I'm not sure, but it could have been because the café around the corner from the stage door served it.

I normally have the gift of the gab, but there have been occasions when I have been lost for words, sometimes when with friends or at one of my *Evening with Dora Bryan* events in a church or theatre when someone has asked a particularly difficult question. I'm not a minister or preacher, so I feel quite able to say that I don't know the answer. I go on to say that if I did know all the answers I'd be God himself, as he is the only one that really knows. But there have been times when a thought or phrase or verse has popped into my head which has answered the question perfectly. So I do know that God does indeed give us the words to say when we need them.

Truth Behind Bars

❧

Kings take pleasure in honest lips;
they value a man who speaks the truth.
Proverbs 16.13 (NIV)

When I was doing a show in Torquay once we were asked to pop over one afternoon to Newton Abbot prison to give a performance for the boys behind bars. Edmund Hockridge and Larry Grayson were among the cast. When we arrived we were ushered into an office where the prison governor gave us a few rules.

'The boys are looking forward to seeing you, but if there is any trouble for any reason, there is a door at the side of the hall which is your escape route. It's on the right-hand side of the stage area, so just head in that direction, follow the instructions from the officers and you will be fine. They will let you out and the door will be locked behind you. We've never had any trouble before, but we always like to be prepared.'

I glanced across at Larry, expecting him to look as worried as I felt, but there wasn't a glimmer of concern on his face.

'Most important of all,' continued the governor, 'please don't mention anything about the prison or the fact that they are inside.'

We traipsed into the hall, where you could have cut the atmosphere with a knife. We each did our bit and then it was Larry's turn. He still looked completely unfazed by the whole thing, whereas the rest of us in the cast were a bit shaky.

Larry glided directly on to the stage dragging his white bent-wood chair behind him. He looked his audience straight in the eye and said, 'Well, who's been naughty boys then?'

It was very funny – a classic moment, and something I've never forgotten, and I don't expect the boys behind bars did either!

I liked the fact that Larry didn't mess about trying to pretend that they weren't in prison. He said it like it was, and the inmates accepted him because of that.

Are we tempted to avoid the truth when it hurts?

Words Alive

❦

And God said, 'Let there be light,' and there was light.
Genesis 1.3 (NIV)

The power of words is quite astonishing. That school play-ground saying, 'Sticks and stones will break my bones but words will never hurt me,' must be one of the biggest lies of all time! Words can be terribly destructive. I've heard it said that it takes about ten positive words to cancel out a negative one.

In the past I've been upset at some of the things the press have said about me. 'The blonde has a funny face and a walk to match!' said one.

Having a bad review is soul-destroying, particularly in the theatre when you have to go on stage and face the audience the next night.

Fortunately God gave us a great example to follow when he used his words to create the world rather than destroy it. So shouldn't we be able to do the same?

Always Available

That same day Jesus left the house
and went to the lake side, where he sat down to teach.
The crowd that gathered around him was so large
that he got into a boat and sat in it,
while the crowd stood on the shore.
He used parables to tell them many things.

Matthew 13.1–3

Working with the late great Larry Grayson was always good fun, but there were times when we both found that being a celebrity was hard work. We were quite used to the demands from the public for autographs and having photographs taken after a show, even though we were pretty exhausted. This comes with the job.

One Christmas we were in *Goldilocks and the Three Bears*. I played the lady who owned the circus, Larry was the ringmaster, and the three bears were actors in skins. At one point I had to say: 'Oh dear, I've got to sell the bears!'

Normally the audience would shout out, 'No, please don't sell the bears!'

'I've got to,' was my reply, 'Because I've got no money.'

During one performance a little boy stood up and shouted out, 'Yes, sell them. They smell!'

I was horrified to see that this little boy was William, my son. Naughty Larry had told him to say it.

One afternoon, after a matinee performance, I was in my dressing room having a cup of tea when the theatre manager appeared.

'We've got some rather unruly children out front because their transport has broken down. We're trying to keep them quiet while they wait for another coach to come and take them home, and I wondered if you and Larry would come and say hello?'

'Come on, Larry,' I said. 'We'd better go and see what we can do.'

They were *really* unruly children, apparently from a children's home in a very rough area. As soon as they saw Larry and me they shouted, 'We don't want to see you two, we want to see the bears!'

'I'm afraid you can't see the bears,' we tried to explain. 'They've gone for their tea.' But it was no use. They just went on and on about wanting to see the bears.

Eventually Larry, who didn't have as much patience as me, got very annoyed. 'I said you can't see the bears!' he snorted.

'No, you really can't,' said I supportively.

'Well, can we just see Baby Bear, then?' they persisted.

'No!' shouted Larry.

'Why not?' was the indignant reply.

'Because she's in her dressing room and she's drunk!' Larry finally bellowed.

Jesus knew what it was like to be a celebrity. He was followed everywhere and demands were constantly made on him. However, he never turned anyone away, and always had time for people. He still has time for you and me. He's ready to listen to us at each moment of our day. Why? Because he loves us.

It's a Christmas Thing

And so they left, and on their way they saw the same star they had seen in the east. When they saw it, how happy they were, what joy was theirs! It went ahead of them until it stopped over the place where the child was. They went into the house and when they saw the child with his mother Mary, they knelt down and worshipped him.

Matthew 2.9–11

I'm not very good at writing poetry myself, but I love performing it, particularly if it's got a comic edge to it. Here's a poem with a double edge that was sent to me recently. It's ironic that Christmas was intended to be a joyful time of celebration, and we seem to have turned it into a commercial nightmare of pressure and exhaustion. Sometimes I wish we could turn the false Christmas back into the real one, as this poem does.

C is for Credit cards that make buying a wheeze.
H is for Headache when your cards are seized.
R is for Remembering everyone on your list.
I is for Insulted when your gifts are dismissed.
S is for Stressed when you find you're in debt.
T is for the Truckloads of presents you get.
M is for your Massive stomach on Christmas Day.
A is for the Awful feeling that you've gone astray.
S is for your Sorrow and the tears you'll display.

And now the . . . **True Christmas Poem**:

C is for the Christ child lying in a manger.
H is for the Holy One who saved us all from danger.
R is to Remember Him who died that we may live.
I is to Inspire us that we may always give.
S is for joyful Songs and sacred hymns that praise.
T is to Thank the Lord for showing us the way.
M is for the Miracles that bless us each day.
A is for the Almighty who always puts us first.
S is for the Shepherd who guides us on earth.

A Prayer for Easter Day

ঔৡৡ

He is risen.
Mark 16.6 (KJV)

Easter Day is the most important time of year for me. Here is a prayer by Christine Odell that says it all:

God of surprises,
we worship you now
as we celebrate the best surprise of all.
The Lord is risen: **He is risen indeed! Alleluia!**

As his present day disciples,
we have walked with Jesus
through the gospel stories;
listening to his teaching,
witnessing his healing
and coming to know him in our hearts.
And then we saw him taken away,
cruelly treated and killed.
Black night fell on our souls
until the sun rose on Easter Day.
The Lord is risen: **He is risen indeed! Alleluia!**

God of hope,
our faith in you is restored:

we know that not even evil and death
can separate us from your love.
The Lord is risen: **He is risen indeed! Alleluia!**

God of joy,
there is laughter on our lips
and deep peace in our hearts
as we greet our beloved risen Jesus.
The Lord is risen: **He is risen indeed! Alleluia!**

God of love,
in Jesus you have done for us
more than we could expect or understand.
In thanks, we offer ourselves to you.
The Lord is risen: **He is risen indeed! Alleluia!**

God of our salvation,
with the help of your Holy Spirit
we will share with the world, by word and deed,
the Good News of our risen Saviour.
The Lord is risen: **He is risen indeed! Alleluia!**

Acceptance

*Accept one another, then, for the glory of God,
as Christ has accepted you.*
Romans 15.7

One lovely Irish nanny I employed insisted on wearing the full uniform and so looked more like a nurse from a *Carry On* film than a children's minder. She was also extremely eccentric. I didn't realize the full extent of this until we had to travel up to Manchester with the family for a Christmas season I was doing.

I had suspected early on that she had a false leg, because she had difficulty lifting her right leg up and over every time she sat down, and the whole appendage just didn't look right. After the long journey up north with our budgie in its cage on her lap, she couldn't get out of the car because her leg had locked into position. It took a while for a masseuse to relieve the clamped muscles and allow her to escape from the vehicle.

On her day off she was having a lie-in and I took her up a cup of tea. I discovered her sitting up in bed wearing my husband's old vest and underpants. Apparently she had forgotten to pack any pyjamas and had 'borrowed' some items of clothing from our luggage.

She was delightful, and the family thought she was a scream. We had to let her go in the end, though, because she was getting too old to cope with the growing children and was getting more and more eccentric.

Does God think we are a bit strange sometimes? Most probably. What's wonderful is that today he accepts me, peculiarities and all!

Bursting at the Seams

Noah and his wife went into the boat with their three sons, Shem, Ham, and Japheth, and their wives. With them went every kind of animal, domestic and wild, large and small, and every kind of bird. A male and a female of each kind of living being went into the boat with Noah, as God had commanded. Then the Lord shut the door behind Noah.

Genesis 7.13–16

I enjoy reading this story because I'm an animal lover and I'm just so pleased that God decided to spare the creatures he had made as well as the humans. After all, it wasn't the animals' fault that God had to flood the earth.

One year I did a most memorable summer season in Blackpool. I was at the Theatre for 12 weeks, in the days when summer seasons used to last that long. This meant that the family could join me for the whole of the school holidays, so I rented a large bungalow in nearby Poulton. It had a lovely garden and a large pond with ducks swimming peacefully on it. When we arrived, the ducks took one look at three children, two dogs, a cat, a budgerigar and our nanny and took immediate flight. We didn't see another duck all summer.

We had a great summer, but all too soon it was time to return home to Brighton. 'How on earth am I going to get the family home with all the extra bikes and swings and things they have accumulated over the holidays?' I said to Joe Dillon one day, a friend we had made during the season. Joe provided all sorts of vehicles for Granada Television to use in their films, so he told me not to worry. 'I can deal with that,' he said.

The following Sunday a huge 1923 black ambulance pulled up outside the bungalow. Joe opened up the back doors with a big grin on his face. 'You'll get everything inside here!' he said, and he was right. We all bundled inside something that reminded me of the old Black Marias police used to transport criminals about in.

Somehow we all squeezed in, but you can imagine the mayhem inside with children, dogs, cat, budgie, and bikes all vying for space. It was like a Noah's Ark on wheels driving down the M1. The old ambulance could only go about 30 miles an hour, so it took hours to get home, by which time it was dark.

Next morning the neighbours must have had a shock to see the ancient black ambulance outside our house. I had a lot of explaining to do over the following few days, and after that long journey home I certainly have every sympathy with Noah and his wife!

The Second Ten Commandments

❦

These are all the laws that the Lord your God commanded me to teach you. Obey them in the land that you are about to enter and occupy. As long as you live, you and your descendants are to honour the Lord your God and obey all his laws that I am giving you, so that you may live in that land a long time.

Deuteronomy 6.1–2

Laws are normally there for our protection. If I break one, like going through a red traffic light, then I have to pay the consequences. So it is with God's laws, which are there to keep us safe. But here is an additional and amusing set of commandments especially for today's world:

I. Thou shall not worry, for worry is the most unproductive of all human activities.

II. Thou shall not be fearful, for most of the things we fear never come to pass.

III. Thou shall not cross bridges before you come to them, for no one yet has succeeded in accomplishing this.

IV. Thou shall face each problem as it comes. You can only handle one at a time anyway.

V. Thou shall not take problems to bed with you, for they make very poor bedfellows.

VI. Thou shall not borrow other people's problems. They can care for them better than you can.

VII. Thou shall not try to relive yesterday for good or ill, it is gone for ever. Concentrate on what is happening in your life and be happy now!

VIII. Thou shall be a good listener, for only when you listen do you hear ideas different from your own. It is hard to learn something new when you are talking, and some people do know more than you do.

IX. Thou shall not become 'bogged down' by frustration, for 90 per cent of it is rooted in self-pity and will only interfere with positive action.

X. Thou shall count thy blessings, never overlooking the small ones, for a lot of small blessings add up to a big one.

Learning to Fly

❧

Consider yourselves fortunate when all kinds of trials come your way, for you know that when your faith succeeds in facing such trials, the result is the ability to endure.

James 1.2–3

We spend so much time trying to avoid life's struggles, don't we? Perhaps this memo from God reminds us that there is always something to be joyful about despite our problems;

MEMO FROM GOD

To: YOU
Date: TODAY
From: THE BOSS
Subject: YOURSELF
Reference: LIFE

I am God. Today I will be handling all of your problems. Please remember that I do not need your help.

If life happens to deliver a situation to you that you cannot handle, do not attempt to resolve it. Kindly put it in the SFGTD (something for God to do) box. It will be addressed in My time, not yours. Once the matter is placed into the box, do not hold on to it.

If you find yourself stuck in traffic: Don't despair. There

are people in this world for whom driving is an unheard of privilege.

Should you have a bad day at work: Think of the man who has been out of work for years.

Should you despair over a relationship gone bad: Think of the person who has never known what it's like to love and be loved in return.

Should you grieve the passing of another weekend: Think of the woman in dire straits, working 12 hours a day, seven days a week to feed her children.

Should your car break down, leaving you miles away from assistance: Think of the paraplegic who would love the opportunity to take that walk.

Should you notice a new grey hair in the mirror: Think of the cancer patient in chemotherapy who wishes she had hair to examine.

Should you find yourself at a loss and pondering what life is all about, asking, what is my purpose: Be thankful. There are those who didn't live long enough to get the opportunity.

Should you find yourself the victim of other people's bitterness, ignorance, smallness or insecurities: Remember, things could be worse. You could be them!!!!

A Heavenly Encore

❧

When I was a child, my speech, feelings, and thinking were all those of a child; now that I have grown up, I have no more use for childish ways. What we see now is like a dim image in a mirror; then we shall see face to face. What I know now is only partial; then it will be complete – as complete as God's knowledge of me.
1 Corinthians 13.11–12

Jill, a schoolteacher friend of mine, asked her class one day what they thought heaven would be like.

'Heaven?' said one little boy. 'Oh, I've been there. We went with my friend Dermot last Easter.'

'Really?' said Jill, with inquisitive eyes. 'You didn't tell me that.'

'Oh, yes,' explained the little boy, 'we went on an aeroplane. But we didn't get out 'cos there was nowhere to sit.'

He must have looked out of the window of the plane and thought because all he could see were clouds, it must be heaven. He knew it was a lovely place to go, and something to look forward to.

It's an engaging story and reminds me how we sometimes get our thoughts about God quite wrong. We only know part of the story so far; I suppose it's a bit like going to a pantomime and leaving at the interval, thinking that was the end of the story. The exciting bit is going back to see what happens in the end. How does the evil baddie get defeated? Can the villagers be set free from the giant? Will the princess be united with her prince? Act II is often so much more exciting than Act I, so why do we sometimes live life as if there's no second half?

That's Funny

❦

I don't do the good I want to do;
instead, I do the evil that I do not want to do.
Romans 7.19

It's true; we do get our wires crossed sometimes, don't we?
Here's a funny prayer:

Dear Lord,

Isn't it funny, how we believe what the newspapers say,
but question what the Bible says?

Isn't it funny, how everyone wants to go to heaven provided they don't have to believe, think, say, or do anything
the Bible says?

Isn't it funny, how I can be more worried about what
other people think of me than what you think of me?

Please help me to get my priorities right today.

Amen.

Leaning in the Right Direction

Do not store up riches for yourselves here on earth, where moths and rust destroy, and robbers break in and steal. Instead store up riches for yourselves in heaven, where moths and rust cannot destroy and robbers cannot break in and steal. For your heart will always be where your riches are.

Matthew 6.19–21

Many people think that because I'm in the entertainment business I must be a millionaire. Far from it! Over the years I have been blessed with earning good steady money, but I have been the main breadwinner. There was one time in our lives when the income suddenly stopped altogether. We had invested our savings in a hotel business called Clarges, which included a health club with a special hydrotherapy pool. It was very popular for a time, but then fewer people started to come to Brighton for holidays, preferring cheap package holidays abroad, and the business slowed down. We decided to turn the hotel into flats, because of its prime position on the sea front. The bank supported our decision and provided the finance to do the conversion. After a year the property market crashed and the price of the flats plummeted before we could sell them. We had to go into liquidation.

We lost all our investment. It was so bad that even today, many years later, we still feel the effect of that financial loss. It just means I should never rely on money, even when society around me tells me that I ought to.

It's a strange world, but thank the Lord he is not as complicated as the financial institutions that seem to rule our lives. He simply suggests we lean on him rather than anything else.

How Would You Know?

❦

What, then, can I hope for, Lord?
I put my hope in you.
Psalm 39.7

I love this set of verses. It helps us put our trials in perspective.

God Wants to Know:

If you never felt pain,
Then how would you know that I'm a Healer?
If you never went through anything,
How would you know that I'm a Deliverer?
If you never had a trial,
How could you call yourself an Overcomer?
If you never felt sadness,
How would you know that I'm a Comforter?
If you never made a mistake,
How would you know that I'm Forgiving?
If you knew all,
How would you know that I will answer your questions?
If you never were in trouble,
How would you know that I will come to your rescue?
If you never were broken,
How would you know that I can make you whole?

If you never had a problem,
How would you know that I can solve them?
If you never had any suffering,
How would you know what I went through?
If you never went through the fire,
Then how would you become pure?
If I gave you all things,
How would you appreciate them?
If I never corrected you,
How would you know that I love you?
If you had all power,
Then how would you learn to depend on Me?
If your life was perfect.
Then what would you need Me for?

Making an Entrance

❧

There are many rooms in my Father's house,
and I am going to prepare a place for you.
I would not tell you this if it were not so.
And after I go and prepare a place for you,
I will come back and take you to myself,
so that you will be where I am.

John 14.2–3

One of my most enduring memories of a lifetime in show business was the way in which I would come on stage each night in the musical *Hello, Dolly!* It afforded any actress the best entrance ever contrived. For three years, eight times a week, I would stand at the top of a huge and elegant flight of stairs and sing:

'Hello, Harry! Well hello, Louie! It's so nice to be back home where I belong!'

I wore the most beautiful costume of red satin with jet black beads, and a headdress of feathers. Slowly I would descend the stairs, through a line of immaculately dressed waiters and passed by the hand from one to the next until I reached the level of the stage. It was the most theatrically magical moment of my career, presented in the most grandiose of London's splendid venues, the Theatre Royal, Drury Lane.

Naturally *Hello, Dolly!* has to be my favourite show and Dolly my favourite character. The entrance is all about Dolly arriving back home after being away for a long time and she is thrilled to be back among those she loves.

The set was a very grand and magnificent restaurant. It would always remind me that those of us who love God will eventually find our way directly into his presence, with him in heaven, that most wonderful place.

Sometimes I really can't wait to see that most breathtaking mansion God has prepared for us. It's probably got the highest flight of golden steps I can ever imagine, and my Lord and saviour will be waiting for me to arrive, with a huge smile on his face. I shall be excited, honoured and maybe nervous to be meeting my Lord and King. Perhaps in humility I will stand at the top and once more sing, 'It's so nice to be back home where I belong!'

Heaven's Gain

And God will wipe away every tear from their eyes.
Revelation 7.17

Losing my premature babies were some of the blackest moments of my life and affected me for many years. But the death of my little girl Georgina at the age of 35 was the worst time of all. It seemed so cruel, and her death affected not only our family but also her friends. I can easily weep when I think of her because I miss her so much.

We adopted Georgina when she was only ten days old, although because she had feeding problems we didn't actually take her home until she was five weeks old. She was the most beautiful baby; when I was in the park with her one day, an actor friend came up, stared into her pram and said, 'That's not a baby. That's an angel.'

We knew a little bit of her background. Her father was a concert pianist and her mother an Australian ballerina. An anonymous letter I received many years ago, when Georgina was about six years old, said that the writer was sure that we had their son's little girl, and that they felt Georgina couldn't have gone to a better home. Georgina's father had not wanted to see the baby adopted, said the letter, but her mother had, and so that was what happened – he had no choice in the matter. I kept that letter, and when Gina was old enough to appreciate it I gave it to her.

Georgina and I had a sometimes difficult relationship because she resented her real mother giving her away. It was one of the 'demons' that she had to fight throughout her life.

She was aware that both her mother and her father were performers by profession and she wanted to follow me into the world of acting. She did so with some success but never really reached the heights she thought she was capable of.

The deep struggles inside her brought about cycles of binge drinking, which eventually resulted in serious stomach ulcers. Sadly she refused the doctor's warnings to cut down and after one bout of drinking she suffered a stomach haemorrhage. She was in intensive care for some time until she was well enough to be transferred to an open hospital. Unfortunately from there she went straight around the corner and into the pub. A few months later she was back in hospital, and passed away. Personally I am convinced she died of a broken heart.

I truly believe she is happier where she is. She has no more demons to fight; she just relaxed into Jesus' arms, taking her joy and beauty with her, but left us with such happy memories. Jack Tinker, the well-known writer and theatre critic, sent me a card which read: 'Don't think of her as a life interrupted, but as a life completed.' I still find comfort from those words.

A Closer Walk

Come near to God,
and he will come near to you.
James 4.8

This old hymn, written by an unknown author, is one that I love. It reminds me of the fact that the more I walk with the Lord, the closer I am and the stronger I become.

Just a closer walk with Thee

I am weak, but Thou art strong;
Jesus, keep me from all wrong;
I'll be satisfied as long
As I walk, let me walk close to Thee.

Just a closer walk with Thee,
Grant it, Jesus, is my plea,
Daily walking close to Thee,
Let it be, dear Lord, let it be.

Through this world of toil and snares,
If I falter, Lord, who cares?
Who with me my burden shares?
None but Thee, dear Lord, none but Thee.

Just a closer walk with Thee,
Grant it, Jesus, is my plea,
Daily walking close to Thee,
Let it be, dear Lord, let it be.

When my feeble life is o'er,
Time for me will be no more;
Guide me gently, safely o'er
To Thy kingdom shore, to Thy shore.

Just a closer walk with Thee,
Grant it, Jesus, is my plea,
Daily walking close to Thee,
Let it be, dear Lord, let it be.

Life is Like a Big Dipper

We are hard pressed on every side, but not crushed;
perplexed, but not in despair;
persecuted, but not abandoned;
struck down, but not destroyed.

2 Corinthians 4.8–9 (NIV)

Do you ever get those days where everything seems to go wrong? I do. In fact most of my life has been like a roller coaster ride. One minute I'm going up and the next I'm coming down. It seems that very little of my life has been on a level, either in my career or personally, which is all the more reason why I have to find stability in God. Whether I am rushing upwards with the adrenaline brought on by performing or falling downwards with worries all around me, at least I know that the car in which I am riding is ultimately secure. I know that in his hands it doesn't matter how fast I'm going, or how much things seem to be out of control, he will keep me safely on the rails.

I don't know about you, but when I go on one of those rides at the theme park, I always hold on for dear life. My knuckles are white with the pressure of gripping the bar so that I don't let go. So it is with God. I know that as long as I hang on to him firmly everything will be all right. I can survive the tallest height and the furthest fall with him as my anchor.

Families

❧

See how much the father has loved us!
His love is so great that we are called God's children . . .
1 John 3.1

I'm glad God created families. My two boys are wonderful. Our younger son William is what we call 'home-grown'. The wonderful thing about a 'home-grown' son is looking at William and seeing my dad in him. William loves boats – fortunately he lives near the sea – and he has a son with Katy.

William is also special in a different way. When I lost one baby at seven months we were living in London and seeing a consultant at Queen Charlotte's hospital. He asked me if we had considered adoption. We hadn't, but we soon got very attracted to the idea of adoption, and put our names down with the Church of England Children's Society. This was 40 years or so ago and we weren't aware of a proper adoption agency at the time. It was still like the Spanish Inquisition, though. We were questioned on absolutely everything. An actress with a professional cricketer for a husband may not have been exactly the ideal parents, but eventually we were accepted. It wasn't long before we got our lovely boy, Daniel. He was the joy of our lives and just exactly the child we wanted. We were so delighted.

What we didn't know at the time was that he was carrying the gene of ankylosing spondylitis, a chronic inflammatory condition that involves the spine and the joints of the shoulders, hips and knees. When he began to be affected, we were told that a blow of some kind could have triggered the gene.

His condition didn't manifest itself until he was 12 when he started having problems with his feet. We just put it down to the strain of a schoolboy paper round at first, but then we saw various doctors and eventually when Daniel was 18 he was diagnosed with spondylitis.

The condition developed slowly, but I discovered that God was already helping. When I appeared at the theatre in Bath, I did an interview with a local newspaper and mentioned Daniel's condition. As a result of this I was told that the country's specialist on ankylosing spondylitis practised in Bath, and later that day he rang me at the theatre.

The specialist invited Daniel to a three-week course of intensive physiotherapy treatment at his medical centre. Over the years Daniel has continued his various treatments, but on certain days his joints are so painful that he can't move. He will be having a major operation soon which we hope will significantly reduce his discomfort.

I sometimes massage the back of Daniel's neck and I've found that the power of touch has been helpful to him and has brought us even closer together. Add a hug with William, and a kiss from Bill and I'm the happiest woman around!

A Prayer for Parents

❦

Do all this in prayer, asking for God's help.
Pray on every occasion, as the Spirit leads.
Ephesians 6.18

Being a parent can be one of the most joyful yet difficult jobs on earth. We need all the help we can get, especially the heavenly kind. This prayer by an unknown author brings confidence to one of the greatest callings that God can offer:

Dear Heavenly Father,

Make me a better parent.
Teach me to understand my children,
to listen patiently to what they have to say
and to answer all their questions kindly.

Keep me from interrupting them,
talking back to them and contradicting them.
Make me as courteous to them as I would have them be to me.
Give me the courage to confess my sins against my children
and to ask their forgiveness when I know that I have done them wrong.

May not I vainly hurt the feelings of my children.

Forbid that I should laugh at their mistakes
or resort to shame and ridicule as punishment.

Let me not tempt my child to lie or steal.
So guide me hour by hour that I might demonstrate by all
I say and do that honesty produces happiness.

Reduce, I pray, the meanness in me.
May I cease to nag; and when I am out of sorts,
help me, O Lord, to hold my tongue.
Blind me to the little errors of my children,
and help me to see the good things they do.

Give me a ready word to honest praise.
Help me to grow up with my children,
to treat them as those of their own age,
but let me not expect of them the judgements and conven-
tions of adults.

Allow me not to rob them of the opportunity
to wait upon themselves, to think,
to choose and to make decisions.
Forbid that I should ever punish them for my selfish
satisfaction.

May I grant them for all their wishes that are reasonable and
have the courage always to withhold a privilege which I
know will do them harm.

Make me fair and just, so considerate and companionable to
my children that they will have a genuine esteem for me.
Fit me to be loved and imitated by my children.

Amen.

My Thank You Walk

❧

Be joyful always;
pray continually;
give thanks in all circumstances . . .
I Thessalonians 5.16–17 (NIV)

Despite all the setbacks in my life, I feel very fortunate. I still get a bit down at times, though. It's when this happens that I have to stop and take account of all the good things that God has placed in my life. A wonderful husband, my two sons and grandsons, a privileged career, what more could I want?

I often find these days that when I feel low it helps to take a quick 'thank you' walk with God. I pop my coat on, tell Bill I'm going out for a short while and slip out into the fresh air. It doesn't matter what time of year it is, there's always somewhere to wander, and as I do so I chatter away to God.

'Thank you for my health,' I say.

'Thank you for this beautiful view across the sea,' I add.

'Thank you for my dogs, Lottie and George,' I offer.

'Thank you for all that you have done in my life,' I declare.

As I walk I discover more and more to say thank you for and by the time I get back home, I feel so uplifted that I'm a different person again. Do you think that God gets a bit bored with our 'shopping list' prayers sometimes? I do. A 'thank you' list is much nicer.

Off-Stage

❧

Let us not give up the habit of meeting together, as some are doing.
Instead, let us encourage one another all the more,
since you see that the Day of the Lord is coming nearer.
Hebrews 10.25

There's nothing actors like to do more after a show than have a nice meal, especially in the company of other performers. It might be late at night, but then we do everything topsy-turvy in this business. We go to work when everyone else is coming home and go to bed when everyone else is getting up!

I have much to thank Nigel Goodwin for. He, with Cliff Richard and David Winter, was a founder of the Arts Centre Group, set up to encourage the link between the arts and the church in the late 1970s. A telephone call or a visit from Nigel was often extremely timely, just when I needed a prayer or one of his wonderfully big hugs.

When I was appearing in G. B. Shaw's *The Apple Cart* at London's Haymarket Theatre in the 1990s, I was very fortunate because Christians in Entertainment were running their late-night restaurant for performers, Off-Stage, every Friday night just off Leicester Square. Off-Stage was run by Chris Gidney and his wife Trinity and it was perfect timing for me because I used to stay over in London on a Friday as I had the Saturday matinee the next day.

Chris founded Christians in Entertainment in 1982 to

provide people in the busy world of showbiz with good fellowship and some spiritual food. Hebrews 10.25 is their mission verse. Chris travels around the country offering what he calls a 'spiritual meals on wheels service'! Often it's difficult to get to church when I am away working or when on tour, so a visit from Chris is like having the church brought to me, and it's been a spiritual life-saver at times too!

Off-Stage presented a wonderful opportunity to relax with other performers from the West End. We had visitors from *Evita*, *42nd Street*, *Buddy* and lots of other shows. Some were Christians, some not, all with varying degrees of experience and understanding of God. We could chat, listen and debate about any subject under the sun over some good food and a bottle of wine, something you can't do at an average Sunday morning service!

Christians in Entertainment still runs meetings in the West End and will soon be celebrating 25 years of backstage Bible studies. One currently meets on *Phantom of the Opera* each week. They call it the Phantom Bible Study which makes it sound like it's difficult to find! What's not difficult is realizing how important fellowship is for all of us, and why we are advised never to give up.

Crossing the Barriers

*I assure you that many will come from the east and the west
and sit down with Abraham, Isaac, and Jacob at the feast
in the Kingdom of heaven.*

Matthew 8.11

Not so long ago I did a tour of the Far East, working in five-star
hotels. They call it supper theatre, where the audience has
dinner and then watches a play. The set was usually built in the
biggest room at the hotel, often the ballroom.

The play was called *The Busy Body* and Alfred Marks was my
co-star. When we arrived at the hotel in Beijing, China I said to
Alfred that I thought it was such a shame that the audiences
were loving the play so much but only the well off were able to
see it. I suggested we put on a special Saturday morning performance for the students at Beijing University. The hotel gave
us permission to do so, and all the cast, including Alfred,
agreed to do it.

On the day the hall was absolutely packed, and the play went
down so well the audience wouldn't let us leave the stage.
Alfred and I ended up performing Old Tyme Music Hall songs
for them.

Afterwards I was amazed to find several students from
Brighton University there, and also several Beijing students
who had been to Brighton. They had been on an educational
exchange. It just reminded me how much the arts cross the

age, gender and race barriers. God crosses barriers too, as this old hymn reminds us:

In Christ there is no East or West,
In Him no South or North;
But one great fellowship of love
Throughout the whole wide earth.

In Him shall true hearts everywhere
Their high communion find;
His service is the golden cord,
Close binding humankind.

Join hands, then, members of the faith,
Whatever your race may be!
Who serves my Father as His child
Is surely kin to me.

In Christ now meet both East and West,
In Him meet North and South;
All Christly souls are one in Him
Throughout the whole wide earth.

John Oxenham (1852–1941)

Friends in High Places

❧

He pulled me out of a dangerous pit,
out of the deadly quicksand.
He set me safely on a rock
and made me feel secure.
Psalm 40.2

I am sometimes invited to perform aboard a cruise ship and I had a very odd experience when cruising along the Spanish coast recently. I was booked to do my one-woman show on board this beautiful ship just once, which meant that Bill and I had the remaining two weeks to enjoy a holiday. Of course you're never really off-duty on board a ship because everyone recognizes you. Although most people are courteous I do get a lot of 'Hello, Doras' as people pass by my sunlounger. If I'm reading it can be slightly irritating to have to keep reading the same paragraph over and over again, but on the whole it's lovely, and I really enjoy meeting people and talking to them.

When we arrived in Malaga I decided to get a travel kettle for our cabin. I thought it would be easy enough to pop ashore to purchase one. Once across the gangplank I got a taxi into the town and meandered around for a while wondering where I might get my bit of hardware. Then I saw a store which looked like a large supermarket. 'Mercado Englaise' it was called. That'll be fine, I thought, because they'll speak English there and I can tell them what I want.

'I'm looking for a kettle,' I said to a girl behind the counter. She gave me a very blank look; she obviously had no idea what I was talking about. On the way to ask someone else I passed a rack of attractive cardigans and as the air-conditioning was making the shop quite chilly, I slipped one on and took a quick look in the mirror. I decided to keep it over my shoulders while I continued my search for the elusive kettle.

I kept asking everyone I met for 'hardware' or 'pots and pans' and after about ten minutes I was ready to give up. I was strolling through the cafeteria section when I noticed two men following me. I was sure they weren't trying to pick me up, and they looked quite nice, so I just smiled at them. Eventually I turned round and in my nicest English accent said, 'Please would you help me. I'm trying to buy a kettle, and I can't find the right department.'

The look on their faces suggested I was completely mad, but they said something that sounded like 'Follow me', so I thought that perhaps I was getting somewhere at last. Escorting me to a small room they waved at me to sit down. 'Oh. They're going to *bring* me a kettle,' I thought. 'That's nice.'

I took off the cardigan and placed it over the back of my chair. They seemed to be interested in the cardigan.

'Want-to-buy-cardigan, Madame?' they said in very broken English.

'Oh no, I don't think so,' I replied. 'I'll just have the kettle. If I can find one!'

They kept pointing at the cardigan and I kept shaking my head. Then it suddenly dawned on me what was happening. They thought that I was shoplifting. There then followed a complete fiasco with the men pointing at the cardigan, me shaking my head and all of us getting nowhere.

Time was passing. I glanced at my watch and a huge panic

crept over me because the ship was due to sail very soon. If I wasn't on board, the captain wouldn't wait. Somehow I had to explain that I was an entertainer on board a ship docked in their port and I had to get back there quickly. I could only think of one way of doing it. I stood up, put on my best showbiz smile and started to sing and dance for them.

'Well hello, Dolly! You're looking grand, Dolly! It's so nice to see you back where you belong!' A few flowing movements led me into a tap routine.

The two security guards nearly fell over with shock. They just couldn't believe what they were seeing. Here before them was a crazy English woman giving them a selection of song and dance numbers. They chatted anxiously to each other and I could see they couldn't decide whether to call for an ambulance or let me loose.

They talked on the telephone and a few minutes later two more men came into the room. The room is quite small, so by now it's getting crowded. There are more discussions, more dancing and more phone calls, this time to the police. Two huge, burly policemen arrive and I go through the whole routine again. The policemen escorted me outside, popped me in their police car, and drove me to the police station. Up till now it had all seemed quite funny, but I began to get very worried about missing the boat. Bill was still on board and he would be wondering what on earth had happened. A quick arrow prayer was in order!

'I'm late!' I kept trying to say. 'And I've still not got a kettle!'

The policemen sat me down at a desk and showed me where to sign my name on a form. I had no idea what it was, but as soon as I had signed it, they put me back in the police car. They drove me right up to the gangplank, and escorted me back on board. The ship's officer at the entrance watched me arrive with a policeman either side of me and looked most surprised, but I didn't have the energy to explain what had happened.

I was so grateful to God for getting me out of a very sticky situation. I just went straight to my cabin, sat on the bed and let the tears mingle with my grateful thanks. I was in a completely foreign place, I couldn't speak the language and I could have been put in prison until the British Embassy or somewhere had eventually sent someone to rescue me. I hadn't met anyone that seemed able to help, but I knew it was God who had pulled me out of that laughable but very scary situation.

A few days and a few ports later, I finally succeeded in buying a travel kettle. I opened the fresh coffee, prepared the cafetiere and proudly plugged in my new piece of hardware.

Bang!

I had fused all the cabins on my deck, and was told off for having a kettle in the cabin. It obviously wasn't meant to be, was it!

In the Wake

❦

Follow the way of love . . .
1 Corinthians 14.1 (NIV)

One of the most moving ceremonies I have experienced aboard a cruise was when we were at sea on Armistice Day. We were in the middle of the Mediterranean on the Sunday morning with the sun shining brightly in a clear blue sky and the entire ship's company and passengers had gathered on the decks.

I stood near the oldest man on the ship, who had a chest full of medals from his service in the war, and a group of ex-SAS men who had served behind enemy lines in Italy. The captain said a few words and then I read a piece from the Bible. Then the bagpipes were played and people threw wreaths overboard in memory of loved ones who had died during the war. I was touched to see how many of these wreaths had been hand-made. Great care had been taken to twist each blossom together. Other passengers threw single blooms overboard. As the sound of the Last Post drifted across the still, silent gathering I looked behind the ship at the hundreds of flowers following in our wake. It was a most beautiful and moving sight.

Here is a prayer for all who mourn loved ones lost:

Lord Jesus, help me as I mourn. Comfort me with the knowledge of your love which is stronger than death. Enable me to trust you for the future of my loved ones and myself. Help me to cast all of my care on you, knowing that the grave holds no power over those who trust in you. Amen.

They shall not grow old as we that are left grow old. Age shall not weary them, nor the years condemn. At the going down of the sun and in the morning we will remember them.

Laurence Binyon (1869–1943)

Home Sweet Home

❦

Even the sparrows have built a nest,
and the swallows have their own home;
they keep their young near your altars,
Lord Almighty, my king and my God.
How happy are those who live in your Temple,
always singing praise to you.
Psalm 84.3–4

One cruise was particularly wonderful because Bill and I got to see some of the most dramatically beautiful scenery in the world. We cruised around the coastline of Kenya and it was about the hottest place I have ever been to. It was very dusty too, and I was always in need of a bath back on board at the end of a long day of exploration.

Sadly we had to leave the ship before the end of the cruise because I was due back in England for a performance of my one-woman show. I must admit I was a bit disgruntled having to get the taxi to Mombasa airport and leave this most beautiful country behind. 'Why go back to stuffy old England now?' came the protests from within.

Many hours and thousands of miles later I was standing on stage at the Theatre on the Lake in Keswick, in one of the most beautiful settings in the English countryside. As I waited for my pianist Wendy to set up her piano to rehearse, I watched the swans land on the lake, and ogled at a most magnificent sunset. What marvellous places I am fortunate enough to work in. It was as if God was welcoming me back home.

'Oh, thank you so much, God!' I sighed. 'Thank you for bringing me back to this most beautiful place. England!'

A Friend Indeed

❧

. . . pray for one another, so that you will be healed.
The prayer of a good person has a powerful effect.
James 5.16

It's easy to get so wrapped up in our own problems that we forget to pray for others. Here's a prayer that you can use. Just imagine someone you know – a family member, a friend, a work colleague, someone you have seen on the street – and pray this prayer in their direction. Throw them up to God, and he will catch them.

May God bless you.
May God bless you with unspeakable joy, not only in the world to come, but in this world also.
May your path be bright and full of light everywhere you go.
May God tell darkness that it must flee at your command.
And I pray your feet will never stumble out of God's plan.
May the desires of your heart come true,
And may you experience peace in everything you do.
May goodness, kindness, and mercy come your way.

A Hymn Too Far

❧

God is spirit,
and his worshippers must worship
in spirit and in truth.
John 4.24 (NIV)

Have you ever been tempted to change the titles of famous hymns to sound more appropriate? I have! Perhaps it means that sometimes we sing what we don't really believe, as illustrated here:

Take my life and let me be
It is my secret what God can do
Praise God for whom all affirmations flow
My hope is built on nothing much
Oh, God, our inabler in ages past
Pillow of ages, fluffed for me
I'm fairly certain that my Redeemer lives
What an acquaintance we have in Jesus
We are milling around in the light of God
Spirit of the Living God, fall somewhere near me
Blest be the tie that doesn't cramp my style

Heavenly Action

❧

... if they pray to me and repent and turn away from the evil they have been doing, then I will hear them in heaven, forgive their sins, and make their land prosperous again.

2 Chronicles 7.14

Some of my most recent tapestries have been used to cover the little stools used to kneel on in church when you pray. They have the words 'Praise the Lord' or 'Hallelujah' included in their design, and when I go to church and see someone on my kneeler I like to imagine that my work has encouraged others to have a chat with the almighty. I like to kneel before God as it helps remind me that I'm in the presence of the King.

Sometimes I have a bit of a giggle when I see people adopting all sorts of strange positions to pray. They put their faces in their hands, pinch their noses or cover their eyes as if they've got an awful headache. It's interesting to note that the only position the Bible mentions is 'lifting up of my hands' to God in Psalms 141.2 (NIV). I suppose this position suggests an open and upward prayer to heaven rather than an inward and downward one. I'm just grateful that whatever position I take, my heavenly father always hears me.

This verse also reminds me that prayer isn't about giving God a shopping list or the latest gossip. He wants us to pray because he wants to do something about our struggles. He's not a God who just wants to hear how we are getting on, but wants to be involved in our lives at every level, from simple words to cheering action. So just be careful how you pray!

The Heart of the Matter

. . . if Christ has not been raised from death, then we have nothing to preach and you have nothing to believe . . . But the truth is that Christ has been raised from death, as the guarantee that those who sleep in death will also be raised.

1 Corinthians 15.14, 20

To me, the whole point of my faith centres around the fact that Christ died and rose again from the dead. Without his death and resurrection there would be no point to any of it. It is right there at the heart of what I believe, which is why it 'demands my soul, my life, my all', and why this majestic hymn means so much to me.

When I survey the wondrous cross
On which the Prince of glory died,
My richest gain I count but loss,
And pour contempt on all my pride.

Forbid it, Lord, that I should boast,
Save in the death of Christ my God!
All the vain things that charm me most,
I sacrifice them to His blood.

See from His head, His hands, His feet,
Sorrow and love flow mingled down!

Did e'er such love and sorrow meet,
Or thorns compose so rich a crown?

His dying crimson, like a robe,
Spreads o'er His body on the tree;
Then I am dead to all the globe,
And all the globe is dead to me.

Were the whole realm of nature mine,
That were a present far too small;
Love so amazing, so divine,
Demands my soul, my life, my all.

Isaac Watts (1674–1748)

Being Salty

You are like salt for the whole human race. But if salt loses its
saltiness, there is no way to make it salty again.
It has become worthless,
so it is thrown out and people trample on it.
You are like light for the whole world.
A city built on a hill cannot be hidden.
No one lights a lamp and puts it under a bowl;
instead he puts in on a lampstand,
where it gives light for everyone in the house.
In the same way your light must shine before people,
so that they will see the good things you do
and praise your Father in heaven.

Matthew 5.13–16

This set of paradoxes is a call for us not to lose sight of what life is really all about. In some instances we can be the one that helps make a change, however small. In others we can but pray.

We have taller buildings, but shorter tempers;
wider roads, but narrower viewpoints;
we spend more, but have less;
we buy more, but enjoy it less.
We have bigger houses and smaller families;
more conveniences, but less time;

we have more degrees, but less common sense;
more knowledge, but less judgement;
more experts, but more problems;
more medicine, but less wellness.

We spend too recklessly, laugh too little, drive too fast, get too angry too quickly, stay up too late, get up too tired, read too rarely, watch TV too much and pray too seldom.

We have multiplied our possessions, but reduced our values.

We talk too much, love too little and lie too often.

We've learned how to make a living but not a life;
we've added years to life, not life to years.

We've been all the way to the moon and back, but have trouble crossing the street to meet the new neighbour.

We've conquered outer space but not inner space;
we've done larger things but not better things;
we've cleaned up the air but polluted the soul;
we've split the atom but not our prejudice;
we write more but learn less;
plan more but accomplish less.

We've learned to rush but not to wait;
we have higher incomes but lower morals;
more acquaintances but fewer friends;
more effort but less success.

We build more computers to hold more information, to produce more copies than ever but have less communication;
we've become long on quantity but short on quality.

These are the times of fast foods and slow digestion,
tall men and short character, steep profits and shallow relationships.

These are the times of world peace but domestic warfare, more leisure and less fun, more kinds of food but less nutrition.

These are days of two incomes but more divorce;
nicer houses but broken homes.

These are days of quick trips, disposable nappies, throw-away morality, one-night stands and pills that do everything from cheer, to quiet, to kill.

It is a time when there is much in the show window and nothing in the stock room.

Lord, save us from ourselves!

An All-Time Low

❦

Once again I will rebuild you.
Once again you will take up your tambourines and dance joyfully.
Once again you will plant vineyards on the hills of Samaria,
and those who plant them will eat what the vineyards produce.

Jeremiah 31.4–5

Whenever I feel really low, I read Jeremiah chapter 31. Perhaps it's not one of the usual chapters people would choose but I just love the way that the prophet Jeremiah talks. I think he must have been a builder of sorts because he built up the people of Israel at a time when they had wandered away from God and as a result faced a lot of fear and sadness.

First Jeremiah warned the people of Israel of the catastrophe that would fall on them because of their disobedience. Then he lived through the period when Jerusalem fell to the Babylonian king Nebuchadnezzar, and watched the destruction of the city and the Temple. Then, he wanted to see them restored.

Jeremiah seems a bit different from the other prophets. He was a very sensitive man who hated the thought of this terrible judgement coming upon God's people. He had suffered a lot in his own life and spoke with deep emotion to the people that he loved. God's words were like a fire in his heart which is why he spoke them with such conviction and anguish.

When we get to chapter 31 it's all about the people returning home, and we get some of my favourite verses. They always make me feel better, every time I read them. The Israelites were at an all-time low, but they had God on their side, and he was determined to bring them back into his safekeeping, if only they would let him. I want to let him, don't you?

Room With a View

❧

. . . for they will be led by the one who loves them.
Isaiah 49.10

I was recently part of a very clever BBC radio programme that involved a group of performers improvising various aspects of my life in show business. One of them would ask me a question and then they would act out whatever I had talked about. It was a most extraordinary experience to see my life unfolding before me in such a way.

One of the questions they asked was, 'Had I ever been in a situation where I thought "I don't believe it!"'

I knew exactly what to mention. Early in my career I had been invited to appear at the Mandarin Hotel in Hong Kong during the annual arts festival. The fabulous singer Eartha Kitt had appeared there on the Saturday night, but when I saw her act, it suddenly hit me that I was going to be on that stage the next night.

The stage was in the circular Harbour Room which was right at the top of the hotel and afforded a view right across Hong Kong island, the harbour and to the country beyond. It really was the most stunning view across many miles.

At night the view was even more spectacular. That Sunday evening, after having been pleased with my performance, I received my applause and looked across the sight of the audience clapping, and my eyes drifted out to the lights of the amazing scene beyond.

A few days before I had tried out the show at Oldham Repertory Theatre, which was quite a different setting from the one I was looking at now! For a moment time stood still as I said to myself, 'Dora, here you are, a little girl from Parbold, near Wigan. I don't believe I'm here!'

God has always been a part of my career, perhaps even when I didn't know it. I believe he has led and guided me in many ways and I know it is he who gave me the gift to perform in the first place. He always wants the best for us, and longs to take us to places that will delight, enthral and stretch us. He is still leading me to places that delight me. Sometimes it's 'beside the quiet waters', sometimes it's through the battlefield, but always it's with him at my side.

Disappointing God

The Lord said to Joshua . . .
'Don't be afraid or discouraged.'
Joshua 8.1

'Dora Bryan, you've disappointed me!' shouted the questioner from the audience. 'How can you say that you are a Christian and then reconcile appearing in horror films like *Old Mother Riley Meets the Vampire*?'

'Easily,' I replied. 'It was a very good part, and the money was good!'

I didn't give a longer explanation. I could have said that Christians are better at playing the 'baddie' parts because we are more in touch with evil, we know what it's about! Isn't it part of our duty to shine a light on the bad things in this world? If a group of Christians had to re-enact Christ's passion, some-one would have to play the soldiers who put the nails in Jesus' hands, wouldn't they? So long as the part doesn't glorify evil, but shows it up for what it really is, I never see a problem.

I also think there is a big difference between the classic horror films of yesteryear and the awfully gory films of today. I don't think I would be happy working on something that brings real fright and anxiety into people's lives.

Although I was somewhat of a disappointment to that man in the audience, I'm glad that God doesn't feel the same way about me. Someone once said that God is never disillusioned with us, because he has no illusions about us in the first place! In other words, God knows exactly what I am capable of, and if I fail he is never taken by surprise. He works in spite of our failures.

I often have to say sorry because I feel I've let him down in some way, but I know he just picks me up, dusts me down, smiles and says, 'Dora, I love you, I understand you and I forgive you.' Don't be afraid of disappointing God. Just go out into life with the confidence to know he cares and is with you all the way.

Ark-itect

๑ใจ

God blessed Noah and his sons . . .
Genesis 9.1

This useful little list of lessons from the ark was recently sent to me. It's from Genesis chapters 6 to 9.

1. Always live a righteous life – even if you're the only one; it will be noticed.
2. Plan ahead. It wasn't raining when Noah built the ark.
3. Stay fit. When you're 600 years old, someone might ask you to do something REALLY big.
4. Don't listen to critics – do what has to be done.
5. Listen to what God tells you – your life depends on it.
6. Put action to your faith. Noah could have believed God, yet still drowned if he hadn't built the ark.
7. Finish what you start.
8. Two heads are better than one.
9. Speed isn't always an advantage. The cheetahs were on board, but so were the snails.
10. Don't forget that we're all in the same boat.
11. Remember that the ark was built by amateurs and the *Titanic* by professionals.
12. Remember that the woodpeckers INSIDE can be a bigger threat than the storm outside.
13. Don't miss the boat.

14. Have patience! The ark wasn't built in a year, and the flood wasn't finished in 40 days and 40 nights.

15. If God is with you, no matter how bleak it looks, there's always a rainbow at the end.

16. When God has brought you safely through the storm, don't forget to praise and thank him.

God's Greatest Medicine

He will fill your mouth with laughter.
Job 8.21 (NIV)

People often come up to me in the street or write to me and say, 'Dora, you *have* given us a lot of pleasure.'

It's very nice of them to say this, and I'm quite proud when they do really, because most of the time they mean that I have made them laugh.

Laughter breaks all the barriers – race, age, gender and creed. It's designed for everyone to enjoy, but I do wish Christians would use it a bit more frequently! Our faith is supposed to make us happy and joyful, because we've actually got something real to be joyful about.

It's also a gift especially for us. No other living creature can laugh, so surely that's a good enough reason to realize that laughter is important and to use it as often as we can?

Much of my career has been based on helping people to laugh, and I really have counted this as a privilege. I still love to serve people with a large dollop of mirth whenever I can, whether it's that TV programme I did recently about celebrity pets for Comic Relief or just sitting at home with friends.

On the personal front, I know many people who say they wouldn't be able to get through life without the therapy of laughter. I remember Fiona Castle, in the midst of all their suffering when Roy was ill with cancer, saying that it was laughter that got them through the worst moments.

It's true. Whenever I've had a good laugh, I always feel so relaxed afterwards. This is particularly helpful for me as I'm not very good at relaxing, so laughter is key to me in terms of switching off or winding down.

Lots of things make me laugh. Programmes like *Father Ted*. One scene in which they all go on holiday in a caravan has always stuck in my mind. There were no luxuries in the caravan and they tried to cook a meal on a tiny little stove and it was a complete disaster. I think more food ended up on walls and clothes than on any plates.

I'm not so keen on many of the alternative comedians. Some of them use aggressive forms of comedy that destroy people, rather than just poke gentle fun, and I think that's a misuse of the gift.

Television these days seems to lack the comedy that I grew up with and contributed to. Nowadays it seems dominated by drama and reality TV. If anyone asks me why they haven't seen me on the box recently I often say, 'It's because I'm no good at cooking, no good at gardening, and no good at DIY!' It always gets a laugh because they know exactly what I mean.

At the end of the day, I suppose the important thing is to make sure we all use this special heavenly gift as much as possible. Perhaps we could even try and carry round a few funny stories or jokes in our heads, or even some humorous pictures in order to share a bit of laughter with others. It really does make a difference, and I'm sure God looks down from above sometimes and simply says to us, 'Keep laughing!'

If . . .

❧

The joy that the Lord gives you will make you strong.
Nehemiah 8.10

Our dogs Lottie and George are very much a part of our family, and we spoil them. Some mornings Bill and I like breakfasting in bed, enjoying a cup of tea and porridge with lots of brown sugar and cream. Bill then gives his bowl to Lottie, having saved a little porridge in the bottom, and I give mine to George. Then they get into bed with us and there's four of us there, reading the *Daily Mail*. It's like a little family unit.

I was out walking the dogs in a park in Leeds one day and started chatting to a girl also walking her dog. She gave me a postcard showing a picture of an adorable mongrel dog. It also contained these words. Many people have told me that they have these words on their desk or dressing table because they help them so much. I think the words speak for themselves.

If you can always be cheerful
If you can sleep without drugs
If you can relax without alcohol
If you can start the day without caffeine
If you can take blame without resentment
If you can resist complaining
If you can eat the same food every day and be grateful for it

If you can understand it if your loved ones are too busy to give you time
And if you can overlook it when those you love take it out on you, when through no fault of yours something goes wrong
Then, my friend, you are almost as good as your dog.

Trapped

❧

. . . where the Spirit of the Lord is present,
there is freedom.
2 Corinthians 3.17

Recently I came back from a play reading in Chichester by train. I had declined a car ride as I thought the train would be quicker. We got as far as Worthing and I decided to pop in the loo before arriving at Brighton which was the next stop.

It was a modern train with sparkling toilet facilities. I combed my hair and touched up my lipstick. But when I pressed the button to open the automatic half-circular door nothing happened. I couldn't get out. I thought it must be me pressing the wrong button or something, so I pressed every knob and rang all the bells I could find. Nothing happened. Then I found a switch to call the driver of the train. Again nothing. The switch didn't even light up.

By this time the train had passed Hove and was arriving in Brighton. I had visions of me being trapped in the loo and ending up back in Chichester. I banged and kicked on the door really loud and shouted, 'Help!' Still nothing. No reaction from anybody. I started to get a bit panicky because I'd been in there for nearly 20 minutes and there was nothing but silence from the world outside.

I didn't realize until afterwards that the toilet was soundproofed. Suddenly I heard a very distant voice shouting, 'Break the glass!'

'Never mind that,' I shouted back. 'Get the driver!'

'I *am* the driver,' bellowed back the far-off voice.

I decided to calm myself down by singing 'All things bright and beautiful'. I had just started 'Abide with me' when I heard glass breaking and the door was slowly pulled back.

'Try and keep calm,' said the man in uniform. 'You should never have used that toilet anyway, it's always going wrong.' I was so relieved to escape, I didn't think of saying that I wished he'd told me beforehand!

When I got back home I opened my little *Daily Word* book and was astounded to see that the passage for that day was, 'Where the Spirit of the Lord is, there is freedom.'

The Heritage Fund

What stories you can tell your children and grandchildren about the incredible things I am doing . . .
Exodus 10.2 (TLB)

Recently Nat, one of my grandsons, asked me to show him how to do tapestry, so I let him have a go. He did very well for a first attempt, but I had to undo it when he was gone. It wasn't the doing but the learning that seemed to be the most import-ant. I think that children should learn at an early age how to cook and sew. We need to teach them the skills of life.

Likewise our spiritual heritage is important to pass on. Whether our children take in what we tell them is another story, but at least we can teach them about God.

I was always sent by my mother to Sunday school with a golden threepenny bit in my pocket for the collection, which rarely arrived in its rightful place. Nor did I, because I would meet my friend Margaret and we would buy sweets and go down to the fields and play.

When I wanted to send my three young children to Sunday school, I had to start one up myself as there wasn't one nearby. I asked the local minister if his church had a Sunday school; he said 'no', but would I like to start one? I didn't feel that I could refuse, so I said I would have a go.

He gave me some books to help me and I ran the class in my home as best I could. A favourite story was Daniel in the lions' den, probably partly because of my son being called Daniel. We would say a lot of prayers, all about the things that were important to the children: a pet rabbit that was unwell; Granddad who had cut his finger; a teacher who was sick. I thought it was crucial to teach the little ones to talk to God in a natural way.

I discovered that a lot of the children didn't know what Christmas was really all about. I said that it wasn't just to do with presents for ourselves but was actually Jesus' birthday. One little boy piped up and asked if Jesus would be having a birthday party?

We had lots of laughs, and I learned to appreciate how vital it is to teach young children about God. So without becoming the wrong sort of 'preachers', let's try to pass on our own understanding of God to our children and grandchildren. Perhaps we don't need to run a Sunday school, we can simply tell them what God has done in our own lives.

Just as I am

Then I confessed my sins to you;
I did not conceal my wrongdoings.
I decided to confess them to you,
and you forgave all my sins.
Psalm 32.5

During the interval of a recent performance of my one-woman show *An Evening with Dora Bryan*, I caught sight of my hair in the dressing-room mirror and decided it needed tidying up. It was so hot under the lights that my hair was starting to look straggly and droop down, so I put in some heated rollers to curl it up again.

Before long I got the call from the stage manager to say it was time to go back on stage. I took one last sip of tea and rushed back on stage without realizing I had left the rollers in my hair.

It took me a while to notice, but when I put my hands up to touch my head and felt the lumps I said, 'What's that?' to the audience. It was then that everyone laughed. I carried on chatting about my hair and how silly I was as I pulled out each roller. I got a round of applause on the last one.

The audience had accepted me just as I was, and I'm glad that God does the same. 'I'm trying to change,' I say to God, 'but I can only do it with your help. I come to you today, just as I am.'

Just as I am, without one plea,
But that Thy blood was shed for me,
And that Thou bidst me come to Thee,
O Lamb of God, I come, I come.

Just as I am, and waiting not
To rid my soul of one dark blot,
To Thee whose blood can cleanse each spot,
O Lamb of God, I come, I come.

Just as I am, though tossed about
With many a conflict, many a doubt,
Fightings and fears within, without,
O Lamb of God, I come, I come.

Just as I am, poor, wretched, blind;
Sight, riches, healing of the mind,
Yea, all I need in Thee to find,
O Lamb of God, I come, I come.

Just as I am, Thou wilt receive,
Wilt welcome, pardon, cleanse, relieve;
Because Thy promise I believe,
O Lamb of God, I come, I come.

Just as I am, Thy love unknown
Hath broken every barrier down;
Now, to be Thine, yea, Thine alone,
O Lamb of God, I come, I come.

Just as I am, of that free love
The breadth, length, depth, and height to prove,

Here for a season, then above,
O Lamb of God, I come, I come!
Charlotte Elliott (1789–1871)

Wrong End of the Stick

❧

And God's peace, which is far beyond human understanding,
will keep your hearts and minds safe in union with Christ Jesus.
Philippians 4.7

Carol Kaye, one of the Kaye sisters singing group, is a good friend of mine. I rang her to say that I had two tickets for a show the following week, and would she like to come with me.

'No, I can't go next Monday night,' she said, 'I'm going to the way-in at the church.'

'Well, they haven't told me about it!' I replied indignantly. 'I want to go!'

'Why on earth do you want to go?' she asked.

'Well, I like all those Alpha-type Bible studies,' I said.

'It's not that,' she said. 'It's Weight-Watchers!'

I suddenly realized that she meant 'weigh-in' not 'way-in'.

Silly me. I should have known, because our church, St George's, has Weight-Watchers, AA meetings, dance classes, a nursery and a great café. It's a church for the whole community and seems to be open all day.

This story still makes me laugh, but I think that we all get hold of the wrong end of the stick sometimes as far as God is concerned. Perhaps we need to listen to him and read his word more carefully?

Explaining faith to someone who doesn't believe is a very

difficult thing to do. As someone once said to me, 'It's like electricity. You don't understand it, but you know it's there.'

I'm grateful that even when I don't understand what God is doing or saying, I can just trust him anyway. After all, his ways are not our ways and his thoughts are not our thoughts. Thank goodness!

Too Busy to Pray?
Then You're Too Busy!

Be still and know that I am God.
Psalm 46.10 (NIV)

I've got this verse from the Psalms written in the front of my Bible, along with some extra instructions like 'Sit down, Dora!' and 'Stop it!'

For several months in 2003 I was doing too many things at once. Appearing six days a week in the West End, I would also often be up in London at weekends for an additional solo concert. The daily travelling from Brighton, plus the pressure of eight shows a week and the press and media engagements associated with it, as well as running my home and looking after my husband, the pets and family, became too much to cope with. At the end of the show's run, I was so exhausted I collapsed with depression and was admitted to hospital once more. It took me three weeks of rest to recover.

Looking back over my life it seems that my depression has nearly always followed a bout of overwork, when I haven't given myself enough time to think and pray. Now I know how important it is to give myself space, even if I have to push some other appointment out of the way for a while.

Whenever I think of those busy periods of my life, it's a reminder not to get myself into that situation again. As my good friend Nigel Goodwin once said, 'God made us human beings, not human doings.'

If Jesus had to get into a boat and go out to the middle of a lake to get some space from the crowds and noise, how much more do we need to do the same?

Infectious Faith

⚜

*But when the Holy Spirit comes upon you, you will be filled with
power, and you will be witnesses for me in Jerusalem, in all Judea
and Samaria, and to the ends of the earth.*

Acts 1.8

Probably the most unusual place I was recognized as Dora
Bryan the actress was in the middle of a group of Hell's
Angels. I'd gone for a walk along the seafront with my dogs
with my tapestry tucked in my pocket, and there were a lot of
bikers hanging around the promenade. I sat down in the same
coffee shop as some of them, with their wonderfully gleaming
Harley Davidsons, parked outside. Then I got my canvas out
and started working away.

Suddenly I was surrounded by swathes of black leather.
They'd all come over to have a look.

'Show us 'ow to do it, Dora!'

I've often found that men are fascinated by tapestry. Many a
time I have sat on a train with a man sitting opposite watching
the whole procedure with increasingly glazed eyes. Inevitably I
show them how it's done and they end up doing it too. I imagine them arriving at their destinations and making straight for
a handicraft shop to buy a starter kit for themselves!

One day I was sitting in the dark wings of the stage waiting
for my entrance in *She Stoops to Conquer* when I accidentally
stitched my tapestry to my beautiful rose taffeta dress. I arrived

on stage with it still attached, dangling down. So my stitching got me into trouble once again.

Despite this hiccup, it seems to be quite an infectious hobby among those I work with. On a recent tour of *The Importance of Being Earnest*, Liza Goddard and I were having a race to see who could finish their tapestry first. We couldn't wait to get off stage and go back to working on a flower or something. By the end of the tour, Liza proved to be the quickest; it takes me several weeks to do a piece about 18 inches square. But over the years there have been many others who wanted to have a go at what I was doing.

I think our faith is contagious too. People often ask me how I've got through all the problems in my life, and I have to say that without God's help I probably wouldn't have made it. Then they want to know more about it, and it's easy to explain.

As I understand it, God has called me to be his witness, not his shouter. If a witness is one who has seen something and is then called into the dock to give account, then I'm ready to tell others what God has done in my life whenever they ask. I'm glad I don't need to go round hitting people over the head with the Bible to convince them about God. All I need to do is be myself, in the hope that God's Holy Spirit shines through me, and watch them come running.

Endurance

❧

... being strengthened with all power
according to his glorious might
so that you may have great endurance
and patience, and joyfully giving thanks to the Father ...

Colossians 1.11–12 (NIV)

There have been several times in my life when I thought the difficulties would never end. I was right. They didn't!

Although God didn't answer my prayers in the way I expected or would have liked, he did answer them in another way. He gave me the ability to keep going. Here is a prayer for endurance:

Precious Lord Jesus, Wonderful Holy Spirit, Awesome God, I praise your name, O Lord, for you have given me life everlasting.

I praise your name, O Lord, for you give me meaning and purpose when there would be only aimlessness.

I praise your name, O Lord, for I can feel the sunshine of your love within my soul.

When the people I care for turn against me because of you, I can still feel the warmth of your presence within me.

When the world makes fun of you and I feel anger because of their scorn, you touch my heart and help me to be understanding and forgiving.

When I look at the world and the world blames you for the world's troubles, I can see the day of your return.

When it seems I am the only one left standing for you, embolden me, strengthen me, and show me the legions of others in diverse places who are standing firm for you as well.

When it seems there is no hope, show me the legions of my ancestors of the faith who wait patiently in heaven for the day of our great reunion.

All these things I humbly pray in the name of my most blessed Lord Jesus Christ, my mighty God, and my ever present Holy Spirit upon whom I can rely. Amen.

Heavenly Planning

I alone know the plans I have for you,
plans to bring you prosperity
and not disaster, plans to bring about the future you hope for.

Jeremiah 29.11

I think this has to be one of my all-time favourite Bible verses. It is so full of inspiration and hope. Jeremiah is writing after the fall of Jerusalem, when all those of position, power, youth or strength have been taken to Babylon. Jeremiah remains in Jerusalem in the now desolate homeland. Sometimes I know a little of how he must have felt. On days when the dark clouds seem endless I read this verse and a ray of sunshine always breaks through my spirit.

God has not forgotten me. In fact God has plans for me! He has plans for you too! Plans that don't depend on how we are feeling, or on our merits, but upon God's amazing mercy, and the kind thoughts and purposes he has for each one of us. Jeremiah's message was intended to give God's people hope in the presence of their difficulty, and we can hold on to that same hope, today.

Promises, Promises

I have promised to obey your laws.
Psalm 119.57 (NIV)

In the Bible there are literally hundreds of promises to us from God. Fortunately he doesn't expect as many from us in return; just one – to serve him to the best of our ability and with his strength.

It's what this favourite hymn of mine is all about. 'O Jesus I have promised' was written in 1868 by a clergyman called John Bode. He wrote it for the confirmation of his daughter and two sons while he was serving the Castle Camps parish in Cambridgeshire. The words still move me every time I sing them, and make me feel I can do anything with God at my side.

O Jesus, I have promised to serve Thee to the end;
Be Thou for ever near me, my Master and my Friend;
I shall not fear the battle if Thou art by my side,
Nor wander from the pathway if Thou wilt be my Guide.

O let me feel Thee near me! The world is ever near;
I see the sights that dazzle, the tempting sounds I hear;
My foes are ever near me, around me and within;
But Jesus, draw Thou nearer, and shield my soul from sin.

O let me hear Thee speaking in accents clear and still,
Above the storms of passion, the murmurs of self-will.

O speak to reassure me, to hasten or control;
O speak, and make me listen, Thou Guardian of my soul.

O Jesus, Thou hast promised to all who follow Thee
That where Thou art in glory there shall Thy servant be.
And Jesus, I have promised to serve Thee to the end;
O give me grace to follow, my Master and my Friend.

O let me see Thy footprints, and in them plant mine own;
My hope to follow duly is in Thy strength alone.
O guide me, call me, draw me, uphold me to the end;
And then in Heaven receive me, my Saviour and my
Friend.

Don't Throw It All Away

❧

He is a living God,
and he will rule for ever.
His kingdom will never be destroyed,
and his power will never come to an end.
He saves and rescues.
Daniel 6.26–27

We seem to live in such a disposable world today. We've got used to throwing things away that a few years ago we would have taken the trouble to fix and repair. As soon as the TV stops working, for example, we don't bother to try to mend it, we just throw it in the skip and buy a new model. It's the same with a lot of things.

I was always darning socks at home, shortening dresses and filling in holes in shoes. Even recently I found myself putting sellotape over a hole in my shopping bag. This is perhaps going a bit far, but I do think that we value things less today.

I was given a Kenwood food mixer once and it lasted me 40 years. When it finally broke down it was no good, it was impossible to mend. Bill told me to throw it away so I put it in a skip outside our flat. I felt terrible. I thought how good it had been to me all these years, and now nobody wants it.

What a good thing God doesn't throw us away when we don't work properly!

A Bigger Battle

❧

*For we are not fighting against human beings but against the
wicked spiritual forces in the heavenly world, the rulers, author-
ities, and cosmic powers of this dark age. So put on God's armour
now!*

Ephesians 6.12–13

I'm sometimes asked that if God is a God of love, why is there
so much suffering in the world? My answer is that suffering is
not God's will, but comes straight from human greed or God's
enemy Satan.

Prayer can change a negative situation. It helps us see more
clearly and lifts our hearts to the Lord when the world around
us seems so difficult. However, instead of thinking constantly
about the problems in life, let's go out and tell others about the
one who solves them. Here's a prayer to help you.

Eternal Light, shine into our hearts,
Eternal Goodness, deliver us from evil,
Eternal Power, be our support,
Eternal Wisdom, scatter the darkness of our ignorance,
Eternal Pity, have mercy upon us;
that with all our heart and mind and soul and strength
we may seek thy face
and be brought by thy infinite mercy to thy holy presence;
through Jesus Christ our Lord.

Alcuin of York (735–804)

Whatever the Future Holds

❧

*For I am certain that nothing can separate us from his love;
neither death nor life, neither angels nor other heavenly rulers
or powers, neither the present nor the future . . .*

Romans 8.38

Alzheimer's is a dreadful illness that affects many people in
different ways. My husband Bill has it, and we both know it
will get slowly worse. I feel pretty helpless at times because
there is absolutely nothing I can do except be there for him.
There's no cure for Alzheimer's yet and the thought of what
the future may hold can be quite frightening. At one point I
couldn't even use the word. I just couldn't say it.

Bill will forget what day it is or not know what time it is. If
anyone tells me they have called and left a message with Bill I
say, 'Oh, don't do that because you'll have to phone again and
speak to me.' So it has a funny side to it.

We do laugh about it all. We have to. Every few months a
man calls round to ask Bill lots of questions. Bill gets them all
wrong, of course.

'Who is the president of the USA, Bill?'

Bill, being Bill, just picks on any name he can think of that's
got an American ring to it. If it's not Rock Hudson it's someone similar. By now I often have a large smile on my face, and
Bill has too. The problem is that I often can't remember the

right answers either! Bill is 83 and I am 81, so we are allowed to have 'senior moments' at our age!

The man doesn't give up, though. He gives Bill an address to remember complete with name, street and postcode. After about half an hour of chatting about other things, he says, 'And now Bill, can you remember that address?'

'What address?' says Bill.

When the man has gone we both collapse into laughter about it all.

I came across a most helpful thought when I was reading a book about Alzheimer's. It talked about not only living in the 'day', but living in the 'now'. That's very true for all of us because none of us knows what's going to happen in the future, even as far as this evening, do we?

One thing I have found in this situation is that it is most important to try and carry on as normal as possible. We love taking short strolls together and popping in to a café somewhere for a cup of coffee. We don't really talk about the problem unless Bill brings up the subject himself. Then we are as open and honest about it as we can be.

I'm sure that God will help me through as we journey together and there are others who know more about Alzheimer's than I do. At the right time I shall have no hesitation in asking for their help and advice.

For the time being I am content to know that I can trust God to take me and Bill through whatever lies ahead.

Finales are Fun

❦

We know that in all things God works for good with those who love him, those whom he has called according to his purpose.
Romans 8.28

At the end of a show all the performers take a bow, in front of the audience who, hopefully, are applauding our efforts. It's the same in most areas of our business though the waiting time before we know how the audience is reacting varies. A comedian knows almost immediately after a gag if he is in tune with his audience because he will either hear laughter, or there will be silence! A singer must wait a few minutes longer, until the end of their song, before discovering how much they have been appreciated. If I am in a serious play, I often have to wait right up until the very end of the show before I know whether the audience have enjoyed it or not. It is a wonderful feeling to be part of that walk-down or bow with all the clapping and whistling showing great approval.

Likewise, the final threads of a tapestry are often the most exhilarating. To pull that very last piece of wool into position is like fitting the ultimate piece of a jigsaw into its rightful place. My aim is to finish my tapestry with something beautiful and useful for myself, my family or friends. That's like my own life, really. I want God to take all my experiences and weave them into something that he will be pleased with.

Some of my tapestries are not good, and I know they're not

good. If I've run out of wool I might use another colour, and I can see it's not right. Nobody else notices it, but I know that God notices it, because it's not perfect. It's not the way he would have liked me to do it. He can see the fault, as he can see all my faults.

Fortunately, God doesn't take just the good bits of my life, but the bad bits too. In fact it's more often the bad bits that have taught me the most. It means that nothing we have experienced has ever been wasted.

At the End of the Day

... The hour has come for me to be sacrificed. I have done my best in the race, I have run the full distance, and I have kept the faith. And now there is waiting for me the victory prize of being put right with God, which the Lord, the righteous Judge, will give me on that day – and not only to me, but to all those who wait with love for him to appear.

2 Timothy 4.6–8

I'm not afraid of death. I know that when I get to heaven the Lord will be pleased to see me; but not as thrilled as I will be to see *him*! I can look forward to an eternity of praising and worshipping the Lord, who has got me through my life, every step of the way, and in every strand of my life's colourful tapestry. Perhaps I will use the wonderful words and gentle tune of this favourite hymn.

The day Thou gavest, Lord, is ended,
The darkness falls at Thy behest;
To Thee our morning hymns ascended,
Thy praise shall sanctify our rest.

We thank Thee that Thy church, unsleeping,
While earth rolls onward into light,
Through all the world her watch is keeping,
And rests not now by day or night.

As o'er each continent and island
The dawn leads on another day,
The voice of prayer is never silent,
Nor dies the strain of praise away.

The sun that bids us rest is waking
Our brethren 'neath the western sky,
And hour by hour fresh lips are making
Thy wondrous doings heard on high.

So be it, Lord; Thy throne shall never,
Like earth's proud empires, pass away:
Thy kingdom stands, and grows forever,
Till all Thy creatures own Thy sway.

John Ellerton (1826–93)

A Generous Gift

❧

Every good gift and every perfect present comes from heaven.
James 1.17

I'm going to leave you with some wonderful examples of what people have said about the gift of laughter. First are some of my old friends in the business who are such experts at making us laugh that it's impossible to resist. Some of the others are experts in the medical field, and it's fascinating to see just how big can be the effect of healing laughter for mind and body as well as for spirit.

I do hope and pray that laughter and faith will help you through your life, every step of the way, until you reach the everlasting arms of the one who knows and loves you best of all.

You can laugh at almost anything, so long as it doesn't hurt anybody.
Sir Harry Secombe

Laughter is like jogging on the inside. It's one of God's most special and precious gifts to mankind.
Ken Dodd

Laughter can diffuse most of life's awkward circumstances.
Don Maclean

A joke's not funny till it's been laughed at.
Eric Morecambe

Laughter is a tranquillizer with no side-effects.
Mercelene Cox

Clowns and comedians are likely to have a high place in
heaven as they must be near the heart of God.
Thomas Merton

Laughter is a very important release valve, and my job is to
open it as wide as possible!
Jimmy Cricket

Making people laugh and being able to laugh at myself,
alongside my faith, has got me through some pretty difficult
times.
Syd Little

100 laughs a day gives you as much beneficial exercise as 10
minutes of rowing.
Dr William Fry (Stanford Medical School)

Regular laughter permanently lowers your heart rate and
blood pressure.
Dr Annette Goodheart (Independent Laughter Therapist)

Laughter increases production of immunoglobulins,
antibodies which boost the immune system.
Robert Holden (Founder of first NHS Laughter Clinic)

Being cheerful keeps you healthy. It is a slow death to be
gloomy all the time.
Proverbs 17.22

There's nowt so funny as folk.
Me!

Dora Bryan OBE

After a lifetime in show business, Dora's performances across the entire spectrum of show business continue to sparkle. From her recent appearances in the BBC classic comedy *Last of the Summer Wine* to her extensive theatre shows, pantomimes, plays and cruises, Dora Bryan has earned the right to be called one of the country's favourite actresses. Having seen her performance in *70 Girls 70*, one leading critic remarked, 'Dora Bryan is a national treasure.'

During a career spanning 65 years, critics and public alike have echoed that sentiment. Her early stage appearances include what was to be a high spot in Dora's career, playing Lorelei Lee in *Gentlemen Prefer Blondes*, taking the West End by storm and proving that she was equally at home in musicals, drama and comedy. One of her greatest theatrical successes was when she took over the role of Dolly Levi in one of the most popular musicals of all time, *Hello, Dolly!* Although a hard act to follow, she went on to play nine roles in *They Don't Grow on Trees*, and was invited to join the Chichester Festival Company. Throughout this time, no British film was complete without Dora Bryan: *The Blue Lamp*, *The Fallen Idol*, *Odd Man Out* and the hilarious *St Trinian* films to name but a few, while *A Taste of Honey* won her a British Academy Award.

There were tours of famous classic comedies and dramas, summer seasons, and she was the first actress to play the

Dame in pantomime at the world-famous London Palladium. Other notable productions include *The Merry Wives of Windsor* (Open Air Theatre, Regent's Park); *She Stoops to Conquer* (National Theatre), for which she won the Variety Club of Great Britain award as best actress of the year; *The Apple Cart* with Peter O'Toole; *Charlie Girl* (at Victoria Palace); with Peter O'Toole again in a revival of *Pygmalion* with Amanda Plummet as Eliza. This production went to Broadway, where Dora was delighted to find how much she was recognized by Americans from her many films. On her return home she once again undertook the role which brought audiences to their feet – Dolly – in a long tour of Great Britain. She was the first artiste to be twice chosen as the subject of the television programme *This Is Your Life*.

In 1991 Dora appeared in the Kander and Ebb musical *70 Girls 70*, which opened in Chichester before a national tour. Dora then played Meg in the National Theatre's production of the *Birthday Party* by Harold Pinter, for which she won an Olivier Award.

Her one-woman show has been hailed as one of the funniest performances ever, and her characterization of Miss Prism in the long UK tour of *The Importance of Being Earnest* was outstanding. With laughter and comedy playing such a big part in Dora's career, is it any wonder that her appearances in Victoria Wood's *Dinnerladies* proved to be such a big hit. Dora remains as busy as ever: she recently starred in *Peter Pan* at the Grand Theatre, Swansea before embarking on her latest West End role in *The Full Monty* at the Prince of Wales Theatre, and then on to yet another national tour of her one-woman show during 2003.

As if the awards and tributes were not enough, Dora has been awarded Master of Arts degrees at both Manchester and

Lancaster Universities and, of course, an OBE. Her faith is no secret either, and her autobiography *According to Dora* traces the story of her life from tragedy to a realization that God had a personal interest in her. For Dora, laughter and life have certainly gone hand in hand. 'There have been some tears, but mainly laughter,' she says.

Help at Hand

We hope that reading this book has offered some comfort and encouragement for your own life journey. The following addresses may also provide extra support.

AA (Alcoholics Anonymous)
PO Box 1
Stonebow House
Stonebow
York YO1 7NJ
Helpline: 0845 769 7555
Website: www.alcoholics-anonymous.org.uk

ACET International Alliance
(AIDS prevention and care)
1 Carlton Gardens
Ealing
London W5 2AN
Website: www.acet-international.com

Age Concern
Age Concern England
Astral House
1268 London Road
London SW16 4ER
Tel: 020 8765 7200
Website: www.ageconcern.org.uk

Alzheimer's Society
Gordon House
10 Greencoat Place
London SW1P 1PH
Tel: 020 7306 0606
Website: www.alzheimers.org.uk
E-mail: enquiries@alzheimers.org.uk

British Association for Counselling and Psychotherapy
BACP House
35–37 Albert Street
Rugby
Warwickshire CV21 2SG
Tel: 0870 443 5252
Website: bacp.co.uk
E-mail: bacp@bacp.co.uk

CRUSE Bereavement Care
Cruse House
126 Sheen Road
Richmond
Surrey TW9 1UR
Helpline: 0870 167 1677
Website: www.crusebereavementcare.org.uk
E-mail: helpline@crusebereavementcare.org.uk

Families Anonymous
(For relatives and friends concerned about the use of drugs or
related behavioural problems)
Doddington & Rollo Community Association
Charlotte Despard Avenue
London SW11 5HD
Helpline: 0845 1200 6600
Website: famanon.org.uk
E-mail: office@famanon.org.uk

Institute of Family Therapy
(Therapeutic work with families and couples)
24–32 Stephenson Way
London NW1 2HX
Tel: 020 7391 9150
Website: www.instituteoffamilytherapy.org.uk

MIND
(Advice on mental health)
15–19 Broadway
London E15 4BQ
Mindinfoline: 0845 766 0163
Website: www.mind.org.uk
E-mail: contact@mind.org.uk

Relate
(Marriage and relationship advice)
Herbert Gray College
Little Church Street
Rugby
Warwickshire cv21 3ap
Tel: 0845 456 1310
Website: www.relate.org.uk
E-mail: enquiries@relate.org.uk

Safeline
(Information for adult survivors of childhood sexual abuse)
King Tom House
39b High Street
Warwick cv34 4ax
Tel: 0808 800 5005
Website: www.safelinewarwick.co.uk

Samaritans
24-hour helpline: 08457 909090
Website: www.samaritans.org
E-mail: jo@samaritans.org